Your Life as God

The Loving Light Books Series

Also by Liane Rich

Loving Light

Book 11

Your Life as God

Liane Rich

The information contained in this book is not intended as a substitute for professional medical advice. Neither the publisher nor the author is engaged in rendering professional advice to the reader. The remedies and suggestions in this book should not be taken, or construed, as standard medical diagnosis, prescription or treatment. For any medical issue or illness consult a qualified physician.

Loving Light Books
Original Copyright © 1993
Copyright © 2009 Liane

ISBN 13: 978-1-878480-11-8
ISBN 10: 1-878480-11-1

Loving Light Books:
www.lovinglightbooks.com

Also Available at:
Amazon: www.amazon.com
Barnes & Noble: www.barnesandnoble.com

This is an experiment in communication from God to his children. "Can they hear me?" I mused. "Will they accept me and will they understand any portion of the truth?" I see now that God has the ability to speak freely to those who will listen and God has the ability to transform energy into words on a page. It is wonderful to see you grow and change and it is my gift to you as I become one with you....

The information in this series is not necessarily meant to be taken literally. It is meant to *shift* your consciousness....

Foreword

Anyone immersed in the vast body of new metaphysical knowledge is aware of the virtual symphony of voices from channeled sources throughout the world – inspirational voices that may be artistic, poetic, philosophical, religious, or scientific. And now, out of these myriad New Age voices, comes a series of books by God, channeled through Liane, revealing the frank truth in all its glory and wonder, telling us how to cleanse our bodies, gain access to our subconscious minds, clear our other selves and march back to who we are – God.

In God's books you will be introduced to a loving, powerful, gripping, exciting, and often humorous voice that reaches out and speaks ever so personally to the individual reader. As the reader's interest deepens, invariably an intimate relationship to this voice develops. It is a relationship that lasts forever, and I am quite certain I do mean forever.

Here is an accelerated program, a no-holds-barred course, where God guides us and loves us, and as needs be recommends books to us and even a movie or musical piece along the way. He (She) enters our lives and sees through our eyes, seeming to enjoy the ride as He guides us back to US, back to ALL. Here is a voice that is playful and informative, that is humorous and serious, that is gentle and powerfully divine. It is a voice that knows no barriers or restrictions, a straightforward and honest voice that caresses us when we need the warmth and pushes us when we are immobilized.

In today's New Age literature there is an avalanche of information from magnificent beings of light, information that possesses us and compels us to look at our fears and express our love. In this series of books by God, you will find truly powerful methods for making this transition from toxicity to purity, from density to light, from fear to love, and from the delusion of death to the awakening to full life. You will experience in these books the love and the power of God for it is your love to express and your power to behold. Rarely will you see more lucid steps for transformation. Read these beautiful words and rejoice in our period of awakening, our return to Home.

John Farrell, PhD., LCSW. – Psychologist, Clinical Social Worker, Senior Clinician Psychiatric Emergency Services, U.C. Davis Medical Center, Sacramento. John is also a retired Professor – California State University, Sacramento, in Health Sciences and Psychology.

Your Life as God

Introduction

You are now on your way to "being." You are not only "being" you are "supreme." As you begin to grow and to shine you will begin to see how you are indeed very, very intelligent. This, of course, makes you an intelligent supreme being.

It is good to know that you have this intelligence that you have so cleverly hidden from view. You began to hide what you are in order to show your own level and ability to learn. You became exactly the opposite of who or what you are in order to confuse you, so you could start over and learn who and what you are.

This is a very silly game that you play with yourselves and often it is never finished or accomplished. This time, however, you are going to win this game of hide God! You are going to win and you are going to be exactly who you are. You are going to be God on earth with full knowledge that this is your true identity. You will uncover you and let it be okay to be you. You will stop judging you as inferior and you will stop allowing yourself to go deeper into the lie.

The truth has come to face you and you must accept the truth and give up the lie. The lie says you are not good enough to be God. The lie says you are not God. The lie says you will become in the image and likeness of God, but it does not allow for you to be the God as well as the image. So you see; religion is not all wrong. It just got a little confused about the roles you are playing, just as you did.

This is not a good time to begin spouting off to the world that you have risen in human form and you know that you are God. Save that for the day you are all able to *accept* it. For now, I would like you to accept the fact that you play both roles. You are the creator and the created. You are life and you are death. You are intelligence and ignorance. You are love and you are hate. You are fear and you are acceptance.

You will soon learn to be love at all times, and this will come through acceptance and a strong will to nurture the light that has begun to fade. You see, you are so good at denying the light in you that you almost extinguished it. Your power is great indeed!

So; how did things get so out of hand that you almost totally denied your own heritage, your own true identity? Where did you get the *idea* to slip out of you to create more? Where does God reside in you and how do we keep that part of you alive and well? You will answer these and other questions as you read this, our eleventh book in this *Loving Light* series.

❧

As you have read in my previous books, you are God. You are the master of this universe and you are the pawn. You are playing duo roles and you do not even know that you are. You are not so much out of control as you are out of mind. You have lost your mind. You have lost the ability to bring your mind into focus and accept your identity.

Most of you are so concerned with getting real that you no longer believe in the unreal. Unreal is actually very good. Unreal is not of this plane and therefore has the ability to be more than real. For you, real is what you see or feel or hear or taste. It is not "knowing of feeling through the sense of intuition." It is "knowing only after proving," and usually proving distorts the unreality of a situation or event. Proving can often cause problems, as proving *bends* the cause and the effect. Proving is a form of mistrust and non-belief, so proving creates solid action. It harnesses creation and solidifies it so it may not fluctuate into other channels of creative awareness. Often it is best to allow all creation to exist and not try to mold any new thought into a form of solid energy.

You will find that vast majorities of pain are solid due to proof. When society has proof that something is painful, society sets itself up to receive greater doses of pain. This is what you are currently receiving on earth. Your pain is great because you believe that it is. You are a product of your own opinions and once you learn to flow and not *hold* opinions you will have a greater opportunity to see only the good and therefore receive only the good.

This, my friends, is heaven on earth. This is how you achieve your desired goal of freedom. This is the time for all souls to move forward and experience joy instead of pain, happiness instead of sadness and love instead of fear. Do not be afraid, there is nothing to fear. We have learned how death is a joyous return to the light and how this reality is *not*. This reality is an illusion based on solidified "testing and proving" that distorted and fractured the light to create the opposite of what was true.

This is the lie. This is the distorted mirror that shows a distorted image. If you can learn to let go of your ideas that create your rules, you will find that your reality will gain flexibility. Most often reality is based on mass conception or mass belief. This will all change in the coming of this Second Coming. This will all become nothing more than an "old superstition" that the folks of this dimension once held.

Most of what you see is not real, so do not let it upset you. When you get upset, you allow yourself to go *into* this distorted reality and I wish you to remain "free." You are here to float free not to anchor down. Our direction is up not down. So here you have the answer to all your problems. Number one: There are no problems, and number two: You do not exist here.

Think of yourself as going into a secluded vacuum, where you must don a special suit with head gear that distorts vision and controls your nerve impulses. You don your gear and sit in the appropriate position to *receive* information *through* your gear. Now; as you begin to receive information you are amazed at how *real* it appears. Part of you remembers that you are simply testing equipment, but another part is so *taken* by the energy that is building to create the events you are experiencing through this head gear.

Eventually, the impulse to run or to fight back is great, but you remember again that you are simply testing equipment, so you fight the *impulse* to get involved and you stay neutral. This is how I want you to evolve. I want you to remember that you are simply testing equipment and do not get involved. If the impulse to run is so great, then you must move to a place where you can calm yourself and become peaceful. If the impulse to fight back is so great, then you must allow yourself to fight and allow for all subsequent circumstances.

It is only a world you view on a monitoring system in your brain. It is not real. Your memory that you are testing equipment has escaped you. You are not *in* the actual event, you are *viewing* all events. Get out of the picture and become the viewer. Do not jump in. Stay out and observe. You are not here. You are just passing through and seeing reflections in a mirror. Do not jump into the mirror and become part of the reflection. You are not part of the lie; you are part of the truth. Get out of the lie by getting out of the events that occur. Allow all to flow around you and you will become the observer once again.

You will begin to remember that you are just testing equipment and that you are not part of the friction (conflict), you are part of the calm and peace and knowledge that you are the creator not the created. You are switching roles now. You are going from earth to heaven. This is a slight shift with great significance. Can you handle it?

◈

Now and then I find a great way to reach you. I have come to know that you do not care to be reached, only because you no longer know that you are me. You no longer remembered your connection to God, so you try in vain to reach someone outside of you for help.

Most of you are in a state of searching at this time. It will do you good to know that you have all your answers inside. You only need to learn to tap your own resources and you will have it all. So far you are not capable of returning, only because you do not know how to. You do not realize that you forgot part of your knowledge and now you must remember.

The techniques I have taught in this series of books are techniques that will enable you to see! You will see who you are and how you function. As with any technique, you must use it in order to gain your positive effects. If you do not wish to be helped at this time you will not use what you know to be an aid for you. It is just that simple. I know that you all have your excuses for doing or not doing this or that, but in the long run you will get exactly what you want.

Those who want heaven on earth will have it, and those who want hell will have it. The choice is yours and has always been. If you choose heaven you receive heaven. It is just that simple. The only choice that you do not make is to turn off the light. I have decided to allow light to live and you do not have free reign over my will. It will be done as I have requested.

Now, for some, this may come as a surprise, since some are intent on snuffing out the light entirely. Most of you are simply playing this game of closing your eyes and pretending to be blind. However, there are those who have developed this skill of playing dumb and blind to the extent that they intervene in other realities that do not belong to them. In this case it is best to go back to your own reality. Stay out of the other's creation and concern yourself only with your own. You do not rule and you will find that I will intervene at this time.

So; I have delivered my message and now we all know who is who. You actually do, you know? You actually know who you are and what you are planning to do next. There is a way to find out. Continue enema and diet and channeling your answers. You will begin to know you so well that you will begin to see how you destroy or create your own good. It is not necessary to purchase an expensive system or to spend your entire lifetime in search of a guru to teach you life's little mysteries. You have it all right inside of you, and it will take only a few short years out of a lifetime that would otherwise be spent in pain.

Learn to love you. Learn to love all of you and learn to return to God. This is how I will reach you. You may sit and wonder for the rest of your life or you may begin to clean you out. What have you got to lose? Pain, destructive behavior, judgment, lack of health, mental illness and sanity. Yes! You may lose your sanity and become a freak who is different and believes and thinks for him or herself. What a joy when one breaks free of the mold that was cast in fear.

So; as you go through life you will know that all occurrences are actually your choice and your gift. You will know that you are creating the best for you that you possibly can. You will know that you have taught you, through the simplest methods, how to get back in touch with your own God self. Now is the time to come alive and stop playing dead. Now is the Second Coming and you are welcome to return. Simply hold out your hand and say, "Yes God, I want to come home." It can happen to you and for you, and it will happen by you. You are creator. You are created in your own image and likeness and you are backward right now. We simply have to turn you around and move you forward. You have gone in reverse for long enough and now is the time to acknowledge your awareness and reverse directions.

Can you do this? Can you stop dead in your tracks and begin to go in the opposite direction? Can you turn around your thinking? Can you make what, up until now, has been negative behavior into something positive? Is it possible to go from dark to light? From confusion and pain and suffering to joy and utter bliss? Yes! It is.

And this is how you will do this. You will wake up each morning and not be attached to anything that occurs. You will not be upset by things that don't go as you had expected. You will only watch and listen and observe. You will become so good at observing that you will never argue or debate, because you will become totally objective in your view. This, of course, will take all of your time and you will find you simply do not have time to argue or shout your point of view. And eventually you will completely lose your point of view because, as God, there is no one point of view. As God you see both sides as good, and even all sides as good. As God you do not judge so you do not separate. As God you *allow* all to be and you *accept* all as good.

Now; I suggest that you go forward today instead of backward, and you learn to *see* from an overall view of goodness in place of judgment and opinions.

☙☙

You are not to be so concerned about how you do not receive as you are about giving. Give to you. Give all to you. Learn to love you unconditionally and do not fear that you will become a monster. You are God and the most you will become is self-love and self-acceptance. You are not selfish to love you and you are not spoiled to love you.

You are you and you are love, so how can you possibly go astray by loving yourself? As you begin to love yourself, I want you to begin to see how you are worthy and no longer consider yourself unworthy. You must learn to accept your goodness and allow yourself to be all that you are meant to be.

For the most part you are so afraid of loving you that you refuse to accept love and attention. When you receive from others do not get embarrassed and be undeserving. Begin to see how you love you best by allowing you to receive. Most of you do not realize the importance of receiving and have given up giving to the self. Receiving is *allowing*. Receiving means to allow yourself to see the gift. Receiving means canceling out any negative as nonnegotiable since negative does not exist. Most of you do not know how to turn a negative into a positive, but you will. As soon as you see my plan you will begin to see the benefits of changing all into something positive.

When you begin to change negative to positive you begin to change creation. You begin to move energy into a space that says, "Yes, this is acceptable. I can use this to serve me." In changing non-acceptable into acceptable, you are changing bad into good, and wrong into right, and hate into love. You are flipping the switch and switching things around. You are finally switching on the light of love (acceptance), and allowing creation to simply be.

This will be a giant step in creating heaven on earth. Creation is perfect as it is and to suggest there are wrongs and rights is to suggest that creation must be reshaped. It is only your mechanism of perception that must be reshaped. You must learn to see it differently and this is why I have repeatedly told you there is no wrong or right, there only *is*.

So; as you begin to see how you have misjudged creation, you will see how you are not the devil, or evil, or wrong, or bad. You must learn to see you as good with no judgment against you. You now hold huge amounts of judgment, and this is how you control you so you won't flip out and do all those bad things you were taught you are capable of.

The most difficult part of all of this is your ignorance of self. How can you possibly know how well you have disguised you when you can't remember what you did in past life or in childhood? You have become the masters of deceit in order to cover up who you are. We must get you *open* in order to heal. Most of you want to forget and are constantly told to forgive and forget. Well, I want you to remember and to face what you have experienced in order to see it for what it is.

This makes a very good time to remind you that you are love. Did you remember that? Do you remember how God loves you and how you do not require love or acceptance from anyone, because you are love and you are acceptance? Do you remember how you do not even belong here? Here meaning this illusion, this state of confusion, this lie. Come home to God my child. Wake up and know your own goodness, your own rightness, your own lightness. You need never ask for forgiveness as you are a perfect child of God. You simply got confused and started to blame yourself for something you thought you did that was wrong. You did no wrong! Ever!

You thought you had gone away from God and made a mistake. You never left. You make no mistake. You simply forgot you were king, and now I have you wandering around dressed as a vagabond and you are actually a lost king. It will only take waking you up and showing you who you really are and you will feel very, very good again.

You will learn to love you by knowing who you are. It is that simple. Know you and you know God. Love you and you love God. Pretend to carry God in your body each day, if that will assist you in being loving toward you. You *are* carrying God in your body every day you know? You are the keeper and the caretaker of God, and God is you.

॰ৠৢঌ॰

*I*t is never as difficult as you believe to begin. You are on your journey and you will return. Most of you do not allow yourselves the time that is required to truly know who you are and how you are programmed. Once you begin to take an interest in you, you will have a wonderful time exploring and uncovering your own wiring system.

You are hooked up to this vast system that is called life and you are even dancing to its tune. You are prepared for life by parents and loved ones who are also hooked up to the system. What I have to do here is to break you away from the main circuit of belief and allow you to sustain a certain amount of power on your own.

As you begin to operate on your own, without the connection to mass belief and mass consciousness, you will feel a little alone and outside of the main flow of life or energy. This is how you create new systems of belief. You start your own company with your own way of doing things and soon others will be beating down your door, wondering how they might join you.

So; do not be afraid to be alone for a while. You are safe when you are alone and you do not require all those who would normally agree with you in order to survive. You will do very well as an explorer on your own and you will learn to depend on you not them. This dependence on others is a little out of control, or better put, "this dependence on others is controlling you."

As you begin to see how you tick, you will begin to see how you use others to make you feel good. It is like a drug. You choose who you desire as good enough to be a part of your life and then you begin to *expect* certain things from them. After all, they are part of your life or part of your existence, and you feel that you own your existence and everyone in it must act just so.

If you do not like how another is, I suggest you leave them alone and move on to find what you do like. If you do not like slovenly behavior or an argumentative personality, I suggest you let go and move on to find what you do want. When you stay and force another to live out your wishes you become totally involved in the work of changing and reprogramming that particular individual. You are not meant to change and reprogram you are meant to love. Love you by letting go of them. This is not a lonely way to live; this is a happy way to live. If you do not "live and let live" you will be very upset and exhausted. You will become so upset that you may end up totally relentless in your pursuit to change this individual, to the extent that you begin to blame he or she for not changing and not following your rules.

Let go and let be! This is the most important advice I can give at this time. You will set yourself free and you will set the other party free. You need not change anyone and you need not attach to anyone. You are free flowing love, and free flowing love sticks to no one and no thing. You will learn to love you by letting you be and you will let you be when you have learned how to know you.

So; we are back to square one, step one. Learn to know you and you will know God. Learn to love you and you will love God. Learn to be you and you will learn to be God. No, you do not know how to be you. You continue to work from programming that is no longer valid nor correct. After you learn to put aside these rules you have taught yourself to live by, you will know more of how you tick and who you are.

The rules must go. The rules are draining you and exhausting you. You are very confused when you try to live by your rules and go with the flow. It just doesn't work. Flowing means no bending, or restricting, or limiting by use of rules. Flowing means just that. To flow is to move with the current of creation. To move with the current of creation is not to be stuck in mass belief or mass rules. You must learn to break free in order to flow.

Now; as you begin to float free you will learn to "be." You learn to be you, to be love and to be light. Freedom is most important in this next phase of training; the freedom from guilt to be exactly how you "feel" like being, the freedom from judgment to do exactly what you "feel" like doing and the freedom from mass connection to "be" free. You will find that, as you go along, you will always draw who and what you need to you. This is the basic rule of nature. All is supplied for you to use as you see fit. When you no longer require the use of this or that it will leave and another supply will appear, whatever is necessary for your next step. So, do not try to hold on to what you draw because it is all interchangeable and replaceable. It all moves on that giant conveyor belt and you have all of creation at your disposal.

For now I will wish you a fond adieu and a joyous day!

Most of you are in such a rush to be perfect that you constantly push at one another and at yourself. You believe that the best way to get there is by competition. Competition will not get you perfect. Only love is perfect and through acceptance you become love.

So; if you wish to be a perfect God, I highly suggest you look very closely at who you are and *accept* you just as you are. Unconditional love is a gift of knowing how you are "just as you are meant to be." As you begin to develop more of a sense of who you are, you will be free to accept more of you. As it stands now you are accepting such a small particle of you that you are beginning to fragment into even smaller particles.

As you begin to accept all levels of your beingness, you begin to know that you are not alone and you are not on the verge of collapse or destruction. As you begin to wake up to the fact that you are more than exists in this particular dimension, you begin to realize that you are very great indeed. You will begin to see yourself as an intelligent being of infinite wisdom. For now, you are so limited in your perspective that you see only this small insecure human form. You have no idea how much more you really are.

As you begin to tap into your unseen resources, you will begin to know how you have been misguided into believing that you were, or are, nothing special. You will begin to see how you are part of this glory and wonderment that is creation. You will not only see the wonder in creation, you will see the glory of the creator and know that it is your glory. You will begin to experience such shifts in your perception that wisdom will flow through you once again. This wisdom is an untapped resource that lies beneath the surface in each of you. This wisdom is God and God is coming in and taking over, which means that wisdom will be unleashed in great waves until it is accepted.

Most of you believe in wisdom, but do not use it. Use your wisdom. Draw from it and nurture it. Wisdom is a rare commodity and is often misconstrued to mean judgment. Wisdom is not judgment. Wisdom is knowledge put to good use. Knowledge which is provided and used is never a mistake. To choose wisely is to know you have many choices and to know that any and all choices have value. Therefore, to choose wisely is to make any choice that suits you. You are creating for you and not for others, so use the choices that work best for you. You are living for you not for them, so use the choices that work for you.

This is how wisdom works. Wisdom, as all, is in the eye of the beholder. You are all learning to view from a new perspective, and wisdom will allow you to know that it is okay and even acceptable to be exactly who you are. So often I have taught you to not interfere with the lives of others and to let them be who they are. Now I am asking you to not interfere in your own life and to let you be exactly as you are.

This is good for now as you will have a time trying to figure out who you are and how to let you be.

∾ঞ৯

Whenever you have a situation that is most disruptive in your life, you are looking at your programming. When you have moments of total confusion and chaotic behavior, you are glimpsing your own dysfunctional system. This is all part of not knowing you. It is all part of acting out what you have *programmed* yourself to do and not what comes natural to you. When you have to stop and think about it, it is not you.

You, the part of you who is God, does not react in situations with confusion or chaos. You, the part of you who is God, does not get confused and upset and decide on this alternative or that alternative. You, the part of you who is God, simply does and is. You will find that you need never question the situation. Your situations are simply a statement, by you, of what is going on in you. Your situations are neither a punishment nor a lesson. Your situations are a created reflection of inner turmoil, or chaos, or confusion. Look at your situation, and if it is not comfortable move out of it and stay calm. The calmer you are, the better able to cope with your inner turmoil you will be.

Now; once you move out of turmoil you will find you may create it again in your new location very quickly. It all depends on the amount of creative essence you are loaded with in this particular charge or area. As you release the charge of the turmoil, you begin to see how it is no longer a burden and how you have changed your inner reality by releasing what was once part of you.

As you begin to release greater amounts of charged experience, you will begin to know peace and calm from an inner reality. Once you begin to release enough charge you will be free to love. Love will come when you have given up protection. Your protection is provided by the ego who says, "I will not let this or that happen again. I remember the pain it caused, so I will never do it again." Now, this thing that ego is trying so desperately to never do again is centered in its own distorted memory banks of what may have occurred in past life or this life.

So; if you are a child of abusive behavior you will find that you do not allow certain types of people close to you, and the irony of all this is that those you will not let close are the exact ones you are most drawn to. You are drawn back to the "original cause" of pain, back to the nest where it all began. If you were beat you will find someone to beat you again either verbally, or emotionally, or spiritually, or physically. You are drawn to abuse so you are attracted like a magnet to those who will fulfill this *need in you*.

This is the root of all compulsive addictive behavior. This is the return of the victim to the scene of the crime. This is a fulfilling one's own "self-created-through-destructive-means-needs." This is the return of all of you to the moment of the original fall, the original charge, the original sin.

You are being guided at this time to let go of your fear in order to be free of fear. The original cause of your pain is not always dealt with in just one or two lifetimes, and this is what drives you again and again to earth. You must break this cycle and be free of the "need for pain." You are all in need of pain and you do not know how much you crave it. It stimulates the body and turns on all the emotions and even zings through your soul. Pain elevates blood pressure and gets the heart racing and at times causes the heart to stop altogether. This disrupts and excites your nervous system and even draws your energy from you. You revel in the excitement and charge. It is a thrill for you and some part of you creates it and craves it just as you would a drug.

Impossible – you shout! You would not respond well to pain and abuse, you say. I differ with your findings. You will drink alcohol until you have a hangover and smoke cigarettes until you burn out your lungs. You *are* addicted to pain. Some of your favorite sayings are "do it til you drop" and "no pain no gain." You even use pain to get sympathy and attention. You are so into pain that you cannot live without it. You are hopelessly addicted and you will wish to drop all addictions and begin to draw only joy and love.

*M*ost of what you have learned here on earth has to do with programming. You have not been so certain regarding your knowledge and now you are learning how to unwind and release what you thought was true. No one is in a position more than you to see the truth. The only problem is the veil that you use to cover and hide everything. Once you learn to uncover and be real you will feel much less afraid. Your fear is all part of being without

God. You disconnected your God-self in order to pretend to be helpless. You cannot play the roles of comedian and emperor and businessman if you are God. Why would you? There would be no fun in it, no point in trying to experience something that is already a part of you.

So; you began to play this role in order to hide you from you. You began to pretend in order to know how you could, or would respond if you were limited. Well, look what you have discovered. You respond very well to a limited view of creation. As a matter of fact, you jump right in and become very animated indeed. Most of what you perform for your role is to attest to the fact that you are indeed limited.

So; now that you are learning to be unlimited, you must learn to know that the limitations, as well as the beliefs, are all made up. You may drop the façade and begin to grow in the truth. Most of what you want has to do with loving you, so I suggest you drop the pretense of victim and begin to love and care for you. As you begin to love and care for you, you will find that you begin to respond by growing *in* love and light. You begin to take on a new demeanor which radiates outward the signal that you are well-healed and loved.

You will find that as you begin to drop the role of victim you will begin to heal immediately. This is due to the fact that in playing a victim you are simply learning how to limit and punish the "self." As you begin to move out of victimization, you will begin to see that you are actually moving out of your own self-punishment.

Now; no matter how you have received your pain, I

want you to know that it was put on you by you. All pain is self-inflicted. I don't care if you are shot by a mugger; it was your choice to experience the pain of being shot and therefore is self-inflicted pain. As you begin to realize the amount of pain you have given to yourself, you will begin to realize the extent to which you are inflicting self-pain.

You no longer see the need to punish the "self" when you begin to learn how there is no wrong. If there is no wrong, or no bad, how can there possibly be any need to punish? You will begin to let go of your need to punish when you begin to truly accept that you did nothing wrong; not when you were an Egyptian king and killed thousands on a whim, and not when you were a child and pulled the cat's tail and were told how very bad you were for doing it.

Let go of the programming that says you are bad. You are not. You are God and God is love. You got confused and thought you must be judged in order to control your behavior. You need not be judged and you need never be punished. Please stop punishing yourselves for misbehaving and begin to realize that you are simply children at play in a giant sandbox. You are acting out roles. The cowboy you shoot does not die and the sheriff does not really lock you in jail. When dinner is ready, your mother will call you in to take off your cowboy hat and wash your face and hands. Then you will remember that it was simply a game of shoot-em-up-cowboys and it was fun. Let life be fun, let everyone play the part they are playing and you will soon be called home for dinner.

*S*o far you have learned a great deal concerning who you are and how you fit in. You have learned that you do not belong in pain and confusion and you have learned you are "free" to make any choices you want. You are free to be independent and you are free to be dependent. You are free to kill and you are free to be alive. You will find that you are also free to be arrogant, noble, fine, obscene, intrusive, playful, harmful, happy, sad and even a liar. You may do it all and be at all. You may be good, you may be bad. You may be happy, you may be sad. You may live, you may die. You may laugh, you may cry.

It is all you. You are God and God carries everything and is everything. You choose from moment to moment how you will feel, act and respond. You will find that none of it matters. It is no more important than going to a big carnival and deciding that one ride is bad or wrong while another is good. The rides are all just rides. Some make you sick and some don't. Some throw you upside down and some don't. Some are peaceful and move slowly. Usually they are used by smaller children frightened easily. These rides are boring for those who are seeking bigger thrills and excitement.

Don't be afraid to choose your ride and don't be afraid to not ride at all. You may stay in the carnival and play or you may get out and let the others play. You will find that you ride the roller coaster of emotions only to know that you have emotions. The zing comes when emotions fly, and so you give yourself a good jolt of emotional trauma from time to time to see if you still have the zing. If you have it, you usually calm it down enough to get on with your life and then you try not to wake it up again, because it causes you so much stress. Now and then it surfaces and stirs you up, but you fight it as best you can and try to calm things down.

When this zing gets out of control, you feel out of control. You feel panic, terror, even fear of yourself. So, as your zing increases in its performance or "need for attention," you will be forced to deal with yet another part of you. Now, when the zing is kept held in position it learns to duck certain issues in order to not be activated. You only want to be excited when you can control it and you don't want your zing to go off on its own and create an emotional upset in your otherwise calm existence.

So; you control your zing by holding it "in place" and you only allow it to move when you want to feel exhilaration or excitement. The only problem here is that your zing is tired of being held in place and is beginning to get excited and move on its own. This puts you in a position of not being in control of your own self. You have lost control and you are gradually being taken over by compulsive behavior. You are zinging all over the place.

Stay calm, get centered and allow your body to come back into balance. Just "be" for awhile and stop reacting.

❧

*M*ost of what you already know has been taught to you by others. You have a wealth of intelligence and wisdom that you no longer use. You suppressed what you intuitively know to be true in favor of what you were taught, or programmed to think

Once in awhile you begin to vibrate at a level of highest truth. It is not wrong to know and to speak your own truth. It is not meant to be put upon others like the rules that are often laid down. What you are dealing with is all truth; meaning "all truth" exists, only for each individual. They see their own perspective from where they stand.

So; if someone is pushing their perspective at you I highly suggest you say, "Thank you for showing me what you think about this situation," and go on about your life. Don't try to change them and don't try to convince them that you have a better perspective. Why? Because you don't. You only have your perspective and since you are all God "your perspective" is valid, as is theirs.

So, what do we have here? We have resistance. You not wanting to give in to their way of seeing and them wanting you to see it their way. Drop it. It is not important. You are not here to convince anyone of anything. You are simply passing through.

Now; when you begin to share your perspective with others, I suggest you keep your feelings out of it and keep yourself calm and unattached to right or wrong. You are not wrong and they are not wrong. You see, when you are aware that neither party is wrong you no longer feel the need to have only one perspective. So, if you are not wrong and they are not wrong, there is really nothing to push at the other and you will all learn to live in peace.

This is often how wars get started. The ego jumps in and says how it is not wrong and it knows what is right. Then ego starts pushing at the emotions to create a defense mechanism to help insulate from pain. Most pain then comes from the effort to protect or insulate the emotions and this pattern continues over and over again. Then as the insulation becomes hardened it is no longer able to sustain flexibility and it hardens into a protective wall around you. The wall is your protection and it must come down.

Now; as you begin to know what you are doing you will find that you are being out-of-balance and out-of-control. When this balance comes back you will no longer feel like your emotions are zinging from here to there.

When you begin to use your anger, I wish you to stop and realize that this is what you are doing. Yes, you all *use* your anger. You use it to assist you in rising above situations. Anger is not meant to be a motivator, it is meant to be a signal that something is wrong or harmful. Anger motivates you to move to action but it was really meant to serve as a warning signal that you are in water over your head.

So; when anger begins to rise in you, look at what it might be warning you against. Are your emotions getting too wild? Are you getting wound up? Are you getting tense? Why? Is it really because he or she did or said this or that, or is it because your fear is rising to the surface and you feel that you cannot live with, or deal with, what he or she has said or done.

You are out of control. Your emotions are ruling and fear is a big emotion. Allow fear to know that he is not in charge by allowing you to take charge and be responsible for your own emotions. As you begin to roll with your emotions and not fight them, you will feel freedom. For instance, if you do not wish the company of a certain individual and yet they continue to call and push at you for attention, so eventually, you get fed up and tell them to leave you alone, the problem may easily have been solved if you would have been honest about your feelings in the first place and told them clearly that you are not available to them.

We have this problem of politeness that is very nice sounding, but also dishonest. It says, "Oh yes, I am happy that you called," when in actuality you are not. So now you have a listener at the other end of the phone feeling very good and well nurtured because he or she not only is welcome, but he or she made you feel good and happy by calling you.

I want to teach you how to handle this type of

person. You say, "Oh hi, how are you?" They say, "Oh fine, it's great to hear your voice." You say, "Listen I have to go now but thank you for your understanding." Something like this will do. The understanding part is actually after you gently and kindly let them know that you are not available. This way if they call again you simply remind them, "Oh, no thank you. I'm not available."

So as you learn that this behavior is okay and even acceptable you will find that you may receive a big gift out of each call you chose not to get involved with. You will be learning to "let you be" and do what you really want to do. You will be giving yourself permission to reserve your self for yourself and not for those who believe they "need" your attention.

As you begin to grow "as you," you will begin to see how it is really okay for you to be you without asking anyone's permission. You have all been strongly programmed to ask for permission from others. "What will people think" is a very big fear in you, so you get advice from friends before you allow yourself to make your own choice. I want you to begin now to be who you are. You have been playing this game of good guy/bad guy for so long that you continue to play the victim for attention or you continue to play the villain because it feeds your ego. Either way, you are each meeting your own needs and I want you to look at why you continue to play these roles

Now, when I write for you, you already know that it is directed to you and not to him or her. You use what you know and let everyone else be, to learn their own way. So don't run out and tell everyone that you have been playing the victim for them when we all know that you have been playing the victim for you.

You are not so afraid to be who you are as you are afraid to know who you are. You will be okay once you are completely unraveled and unwound and untied and uncovered so that you may shine.

⚛️

*W*henever you are alone you have an opportunity to grow. You have the ability and the desire to be God expanded in matter and as you expand you allow more light to enter and take control *in* matter. You are not so much in a situation of unexpanded awareness as you are in a situation of expanded intelligence. Your intelligence is there. Your knowledge is there. How do you think Liane writes this information? It is part of her cellular makeup. She is expanded intelligence, and every time I allow more light to enter her body she is allowed to move to the next level of intelligence or information.

As I first began to write through Liane I did not know how her body would react to various levels and degrees of vibration. She often received my charge and experienced great conflict with her own dense charges. This creates a tiredness and an ache in her body. The aches would lead to a discharge, and I found that if I allowed her body to rest she might retain small doses of my *charge* in between writings.

This assisted Liane in discharging her own dense programming. She has had time to reconsider her work for God, but she has always returned for more. This indicates that on a conscious level she feels something very good from all of this.

As I have advanced the clarity and intensity of information, she has begun to *receive* it with less fear and greater receptivity. This allows her own fear to come to the surface and discharge. She takes her daily enema, which allows the body to clear the charge of electricity through the bowels. She is becoming a light being. She is taking on light, and sloughing off darkness, and recharging just like a battery would recharge when dead. A dead battery cannot be used to light a flashlight or beacon. A charged battery is best.

So; how does Liane learn to do this? She does not know to this day how it all works. I once told her how rich her life would be and she believed in me and is still waiting for her heaven on earth. She does not realize how far she has come, as she cannot see inside herself where I am. She is still confused as to who I am, and how I can be God and be in her, and write for her, and joke with her. She is still confused as to why she has conflict after several years of releasing and clearing debris from her body.

She has left the majority of her pain behind. She looked at everything she had hidden from herself and decided to forgive herself for her crime. She is now moving into a new phase, and I wish her to know that she has reconnected once again with the essence that is her soul.

She is no longer separate from her spirit and she is no longer connected to density. She is beginning her *shift* to higher consciousness. "About time," you may say, but I want you to know that you (not I) are dealing in time ratio and nothing *is* for you until it is run through your sequence of time to *create* an event.

Liane is an example of man working together with God in order to save the self from self-destructive behavior. I think we have done well with this process, and Liane actually feels better here in her current awareness than she ever felt in her past unaware state. She is free of the pain that bound and circled her. She is free to create from a new level of thought. She is free to move ahead without baggage. She has effectively dropped a great deal of baggage from guilt, judgment and shame. She is recharged and ready to create something new for herself. Mostly, she is resting before she allows her heart to reopen, and for trust to guide her life. I allow her the time she needs for her psyche as well as her mind and body to heal. To face your demons is a harrowing experience for some of you.

So; now you know a little of where Liane is and how she got here. She did not get here by denying access. She gave herself to me as she no longer felt worthy. Now I have given her back a new perspective with a worthy outlook.

*W*henever you begin to know the self, you begin to see judgment. Judgment has always been a great part of your lives, and to let it go is to let go of a great part of you. You will not wish to let go of great big parts of you without a struggle. This is the battle you wage within yourself. If everyone says you are bad and irreverent, you not only believe them, but you use this information to base your judgment of others.

You are locked in to whatever belief system you were taught. I highly suggest you look to your parents and primary care givers to see how you are programmed. You may not like what you see as you have been rebelling against your parents for years. Or, it may be that you like what you see and admire your parent's *perspective* and have used it in your own life. This is where you began. You began at home and your programming for right and wrong started there. You were punished for bad and praised for good.

You will find that a great deal of what you *learned* was actually absorbed telepathically and you thought it was you all along. You can take-on parts of your environment as well. If you are raised in a dark, dingy place, you feel best in dark, and dingy places. If you were raised in bright sunlight with open windows, you will love bright sunlight and open windows.

Now; if you hated your parent figure you may have taken the *position* of hating everything that reminds you of your parent. So now, if your friend or loved one suggests you are loud or messy you go crazy, because your parent also said you are loud or messy and you hated that particular parent.

So; how do you know who you are and why you get ticked-off at others? It is very simple. You are a time bomb waiting to go off and each time you re-experience your original pain, you blow a little. Some of you blow outwardly and yell at others and some of you sit in your room and hide your pain. Either way, it is pain and you are expressing it and acting it out. You have always done this and now I simply want you to become *aware* of what you are doing and why.

You will learn a great deal about you by looking at how you *react* to others. You are reacting in very strange ways and it is out of control. Your programming has taken over. The darkness and confusion is great, and as long as you continue to suppress the truth you will continue to live in the lie.

༄༅༅

*W*ell, I certainly hope you are ready for this. I have just decided to write about hate! Hate is not love and love is not hate. Hate is pushing something away as hard as you can. Hate is total rejection and hate is total denial of acceptance. Hate has a bad rap and is no more important in your lives than any other emotion. Do not fear 'hate.' If you hate someone it only means that you totally reject that person as being acceptable for you. You may choose who is acceptable for you as I have given all free will of choice.

When you begin to hate someone you begin to justify to yourself why this person is non-acceptable. Most of you call it non-likable but it is really non-acceptable. So, you begin to dislike someone, for whatever reasons, and then you begin to barrage this person with your distaste. You may gather friends around you who will support your point of view, or you may simply turn away from the one you are showing distaste for.

Either away, the hate begins to grow and is centered in your distaste for the offender. So, what did this person do to make you so resentful of him or her? Maybe she or he wrote you a letter and told you off. Or maybe this objectionable character had the nerve to tell you to your face that you lie, or cheat, or are a slob. Either way it is a case of hurt. Here we go again with this pain game. You all play this game and I wish to expose it for what it is. It is childish and you only hurt you. You think you only hurt the one you love, but you are the only one you can ever hurt by your feelings and your emotions.

Pretend you are standing in front of your mirror and you look at your face and think, "Wow, you don't look good." All of a sudden the one facing you shouts back "You look pretty awful yourself." Now you throw back, "Well, at least I don't look as bad as you do." And the one you are now glaring at returns with, "Well, you know what? I always did think you were ugly." And you close your eyes and hate him or her so much, and the only problem is that it is just your reflection telling you what you think of you.

Please try to remember that when "they" hate you it is only you hating you, because they are only a mirror and can only throw back what you put out initially. This is called imaging. If you duck to the left, they will duck to the right. A mirror reflection is not exact. It rotates and moves in the opposite direction that you move in. This makes you crazy! You *hate* those who oppose you, or are opposites from you on any position. Think about it. You are killing off parts that reflect what you hate. Don't kill... heal. Healing will help you see who and what you really are.

Aren't you tired of fighting and struggling and hurting and hating? Doesn't it wear you down and exhaust you? Are you ready to live and let live? After all, what could possibly be so awful about an opposing force? Will it destroy you, because you do not look like it or see it as you? I do not think so. An opposing force is to show you that you are multidimensional with two sides, a top and a bottom and a middle that never ends.

So, now we have this opposing force and it threatens your very existence by denying your existence or the truth of your reality. What can you do? Do you push at it day and night and try to reverse its position so it will see as you see, or do you *allow* it to reflect you without repelling you? You must decide how to *receive* your other half. Will you reject this half of you, or will you receive it as part of this "whole" that is you?

You will find that as you begin to know that this opposite force is actually the back view of you, you will be most embarrassed for all your name calling and harassing. Do not kick your own butt! You are out of control and you want to hurt someone because you think you are hurt and what you are is confused.

⚬⚬⚬

*W*hen you begin to evolve to a state of complete joy, you will have released all past programming. You will have begun to know you and you will have begun to realize how you are made to look different than what you really are. You will begin to see the truth of this dimension and break through the lie of the veil.

This is how you will *see* love. You will learn to see love by creating a new world, or reality, for yourself based on truth. You will know how you have created all of your reflections, and you will know how you can change what you no longer wish to see. It is all up to you how you see it. Strike a pose and a reflection will appear. And how do you strike a pose? You choose a stance, a position that you wish to take on any topic there is. You stand in your position and do not allow other positions, and there you have it. You will create the opposite or your reflection, and it will return to you. You may see it briefly in another, or, if your position refuses to move, you will see it in others as long as you refuse to budge your viewpoint.

The moment you get relaxed or flexible, you create

another reflection that shows the opposite of your position. So, what happens when you become love and see all positions? You no longer view your opposing reflection, because now you see and *accept* all positions, so you own no one specific position.

This is called floating. Free-floating is total freedom of all attachment to a stance in the field of matter. You hoist your anchor and rise up out of the dense field of matter, and this is take-off. This is your first step to ascension. Do you like how it feels to have no position or no point of view? Can you accept all views as valid? You are halfway home, if this is where you are. This does not mean defending another's viewpoint and it does not mean not seeing any viewpoint. It does mean having the ability to see all sides.

You will come to a point in all of this that you will no longer be able to argue your point of view, because the other points of view will be so strong that no one point of view stands out for you. This is knowledge and wisdom. You have reached your pinnacle of truth and you can no longer *hide* the truth from yourself. This is the moment you begin to *realize* how you are God and how God is you. This is the moment you begin to know that this time on earth is simply *"your life as God."* You wore the crown of a king or queen in the past, and you wore the rags of a beggar, now you will wear the light of God.

*W*hen you begin to rise above this illusion, you will be very grateful to finally see how you got confused in the first place. Most of what confuses you is connected to your belief that you are not good enough or smart enough. Now what I must do is teach you to trust you. This is a difficult one, as you all believe you are right and right only leads to deeper entrapment in the illusion.

So; let's start with wrong. It is not wrong to lie. It is not wrong to cheat, it is not wrong to steal, it is not wrong to hate. It is not a sin to do any of these, nor is it wrong. It simply is. Can you just let it be? Can you live and let live? Can you keep yourself safe without attacking others? Most of you are so afraid of being lied to, or stolen from, or cheated, that you point at and *judge* those who commit these crimes before they can commit them against you.

Your defenses are beginning to kill you and shut you down. Your judgment is so great that it controls your every move and who you will or will not accept. Now; I do want you to remember that you have a free will, and this free will allows you choice. To have a choice is not the same as to condemn one in favor of another. Free will allows for all to be free of condemnation and for a choice as to which direction you choose.

You are not going down a bad, or wrong, or destructive road. You are simply hurting you and it is killing you as you currently see you. When you begin to see yourself through the eyes of truth, you will no longer believe that you die and this analogy will no longer work on you. You see, this is how I channel this information. I say what you need to hear from where you stand, and I give you the answers that will assist you in moving to your next level of evolution. Why do you think I ask you to read these books in order? You are not wound backward, you are wound foreword and now I am reversing you.

So; if you have confusion concerning information that changes as you read this series of books, it is just the level that is acceptable for this student at the time. Say I am teaching a small child about life and sex. I don't come to the point and say, "The penis fits into the vagina," and expect the child to *receive* this information with joy. No, what I would say is that, "A wonderful miracle occurs and a mommy and daddy grow a baby from a seed of love." This is what I have done for you in this series, and I hope you do not choose to quote and brag that you have discovered God's truth, when in actuality you are simply gaining wisdom as you read.

So; perspective is only a stance, and all stances change with movement and growth in wisdom.

※

*W*henever you begin to see how you are wound up and raveled and tied in knots, you will begin to know that you react to certain situations out of fear. What I would like you to do is to become *aware* of this fear and trace it back to its original cause. This will assist you in working through your rough spots. You are creating rough spots out of a need to deal with these original emotions.

Each time you have an upset in your life it is a cry for help. It is you saying to all parts of you, "Let's stop this dysfunctional behavior and begin to love our self." So if you can remember this when you are upset it may help. Just remind yourself that *you* really do love yourself and let everything else that occurs be meaningless.

Most of you re-create situation after situation where you must learn to love you above all else. This is how we learn the meaning of the words *I am.* I am God. I am love. How can you possibly be God and think the thoughts about you that you think? How can you possibly be God and not love you enough to take real good care of you? And how can you possibly be God and carry so much self-loathing and self-disgust?

God is going to be born in matter and whether you volunteer to take part is up to you. You may continue to *hold* on to your pain and your fear, or you may let go and hold only love, which leads to trust and faith. This is how you know where you are. How much trust and faith do you have in yourself? Are you creating for yourself or are you playing the victim? Are you falling into the guilt trap or are you rising above it? These are your dysfunctions. You feel guilty, you feel bad, you feel wrong and you feel you have been wronged. You feel useless, you feel incompetent and you feel pain. These are not your true state of being and they all lead to pain and hurt and, sometimes, even harmful or hurtful behavior.

Do not point your finger at others. If you do not appreciate how someone responds to you I highly suggest you move away from that someone. If you do not, you are not only saying to yourself, "I don't deserve better treatment," you are also saying to that person, "Yes, I give you permission to treat me in this fashion, as I do not deserve better." Your mirror is reflecting what you believe right back to you.

So; how much wasted time and energy do you spend trying to get someone to treat you better or show you greater consideration? You are learning in this class to take responsibility for yourself and not try to hand yourself and your feelings over to someone else for safekeeping. We are all gods here and it's time we took full responsibility for who we are.

⚜

As far as you know you are not yet dead. Of course, you are not really sure because you do not know what dead is. If dead is being totally unconscious to the fact that you are God, then it would stand to reason that what you are now experiencing is death. What is life is light. What is absence of light is death. So... are you now dead and waiting to be born? Could you be so confused in this death sleep that you think you are still alive, but you are simply waiting to come alive? Could it be that you are like a butterfly in a cocoon and you think that this state is all there is, when in actuality this state is simply a brief unconsciousness before you emerge into life?

Could it be that everything is so totally opposite of what you now believe, that you are actually looking at the back view thinking it is the front? Could it be that you are not even yet born, you are to "become" soon and are in process of becoming? Could it be that you are not even here yet, that you have sent your thought forward and it is now beginning to inherit this plane?

Could it be that you no longer exist as you, and in this case, you are God, so you no longer exist as God? Could it be that you forged ahead in order to *expand* creation and the rest of *you* has not yet arrived? Could it be that you were once motionless and in creating friction you began to move, and in creating movement you began to expand, and in the "expansion of you" you separated parts of you; and now the part of you that does not know who you are is waiting for the part that has light to show this other dark part who he is; who the master is?

Could it be that once the light reconnects with the separated parts they will be as they once were? Could it be that all life as you *now* know it is not true life, but is migration *into* a life force? Could it be that you are not so advanced as you believe, and could it be that you are totally lost without the light that tells you who you are?

Yes... I think it could be!

✻

*S*o far you have discovered that you are not all that you see. Now that you no longer know who or what you are, you will find that you get a little less rigid with yourself. After all, how can you boss you around when you do not know what you are supposed to be doing, or how you are supposed to be?

You will begin to see how you have come to be where you are, and you will come to see how you are developing just fine. You are not so much a mess as you are confused. Once this confusion leaves, you will be free to express your true identity. You will be free to express your own belief in yourself without fear of criticism, because *you* will no longer carry criticism.

Much of what you are learning is based on trust that you are God and faith that you create only what is best for you. It is only when judgment jumps up and says, "No, this is wrong. This shouldn't happen to me, because this is bad," that you begin to lose your trust and faith. In actuality, those times of distress are actually the best times for you, as they *move* you out of a fear and into the light.

Most of your trust and faith is based on a willingness to be in this or that situation, with the insight that gives you peace of mind. Most of your insight is based on what you know, and most of what you know is based on ignorance. You are not in the light and you have not been put in this dark place because you are bad or wrong.

You are simply being born. You are like the baby in a womb and you are confused about where you are and what is happening.

Awareness and intelligence will grow within you when you begin to *allow* it to. As long as you hold on to what you now are, you will not move. You are stuck in place by your *will* to stay. Your will to survive is keeping you in this struggle. Give up your will to survive and allow destruction to be a valid choice. Destruction could be the downfall of you. You could be destroyed simply by letting go of who you believe you are. You will find that you do not know who you are, so why hang on to who you are? Let go and move into intelligence and life.

Intelligence and life will tell you that you are 'not.' You do not really exist and everything that you believe is simply a layer that you took on. Don't expect to 'not' be, because you cannot 'not' be. You always are and always will be. You simply will not be this you with this belief system.

So; if your beliefs are so good and valid, I highly suggest you hold on for dear life. You will want to know that good and valid are also judgment calls and you are holding on to something that is fear-based and holds everyone down. Now we have you in a position where you are no longer willing to be good, but you don't want to be bad either. Now what can you do? I think maybe you would do well to simply be who and what you feel like. Be you. Be spontaneous and, by all means, learn to *trust* you. You are God and the more you learn to trust you the more you learn to trust God.

❧

More than once you have given way to anger. Some of you express your anger by controlling those around you and others by being chaotic. Anger is anger and it comes out in many forms. You will find that you do not always *know* you are expressing anger when you do. Most of you begin to see how you do this much later, after you have developed your senses of perception.

You are all on a graduating scale of fluctuating knowledge and you all have the ability to see who you are when you develop your senses of perception. Perception is often how you know you from your neighbor or friend. You perceive you differently than you perceive others. But what if, as a baby or a small infant, you were perceived by your parent as a part of their identity? Would it not stand to reason that you now *carry* information that says you are owned by and part of their person? And if this is possible, would it not stand to reason that they may punish you (as part of them) for crimes they believe they deserve punishment for?

And if all this could be, would it not be possible that you spend your entire life trying to retain a sense about who you are and if you actually belong to yourself, or to the one who taught you? And if all of this is true, could it not be possible that your fear of control is based on fear of losing your own identity?

So; how do we get you to know that you are yours and no one can take you away? How do we get those who have been sexually abused and physically abused to realize that their body does not belong to another, it belongs only to them? And how do we get those, who have been told over and over again how or what they must do or believe, that have been told that they have no viewpoint of their own, to realize that indeed they have? How do we retain enough separation to know that we have free will choices, and how do we know how much of ourselves we have allowed others to govern?

Well, you can start by knowing you and watching you. Do you like to give your problems to someone else to solve? Do you always reach for your phone for advice from Mom or Dad, or do you live your own life and acknowledge that your parent's advice is just your parent's advice? How many times do you go to your friends before you make a move and test out your own ideas on them to see how *acceptable* they may or may not be? How often do you suggest what you want and are talked out of it by another?

What are your boundaries? Who are you making yourself into? Are you becoming another of your parents, or are you becoming a new identity? Who has affected you most in your life? Who was with you most of your childhood and those precious baby years? This is when you *develop* your sense of who you are and how you are *perceived* by your caretaker. Usually, how you were perceived is how you see yourself.

If your parent chose to have a child out of

loneliness and lack of self-love, you are probably lonely with no self-love. The programming here runs deep! If your parent did not want a child and, "voilà," here you are, you may be very independent and very strong-willed in survival techniques. You may even not want children yourself. You see, you learn from those who are your teachers and they've learned from those who were their teachers. And then we have the different combinations of mother/father programming. He wants a baby; she hates the idea, but goes along to please him. This, of course, may also work in reverse. He may hate the idea and even feel guilt that he does. This way the baby will feel not only unwanted but a sense of guilt about being here in this particular life.

So, look at who you are? You are made up of many layers and this is the time to take them off! You all know how to and you all know who you really are and you all know the real truth about you.

❧

You are not so big as you are small. You think you are big and tough and rugged, when in actuality you are very tiny and vulnerable. So how can you judge yourself so harshly for being bad if you are so frail? I highly suggest you use your common sense and learn to forgive you for all that you have ever done. Now is a good time to begin. Start by forgiving yourself for being stupid. This is a very big one for all of you. You continually call yourself ignorant, stupid, dumb, lazy, weak, stubborn, insensitive.... Oh, wait! I'm getting a little carried away here.... And that's just what you do. You get a lot carried away with judging you and how you act, talk, think, walk, you name it, you judge you for it.

Now; I want you to stop judging you by allowing you to be right. We have done this work on others and our judgment toward them, and I have asked you to allow everyone to be right, because there is no wrong. So, if there is no wrong, "you are not wrong." You are not dumb, you are not stupid, you did not make an ass out of yourself, and God loves you just the way you are.

So; as you go to bed tonight I want you to know that you are the best; the most wonderful light in all of creation. "You"... little ol' you are a light that is turning into a beacon for God! How can that little light possibly judge his or her actions? It is like your fairy tale about the ugly duckling who did not know that he was actually becoming a beautiful, elegant swan. How could he have known? He was so afraid he was ugly, but he grew into himself, as you are now doing.

Do not feel ugly my little duckling. You are being transformed with gentle loving care and you do not even know that you are. You will soon see how you are to "grace" God with your goodness and your love. You are special and you are being born to God.

෴

*W*here will you be when you no longer create pain? Where will you be when you no longer create confusion and how will you succeed without the knowledge of who you are? Knowledge is enlightenment and through knowledge you receive wisdom. Wisdom is often what is lacking when you create pain.

For those of you who have begun to enter your pain, I wish you to know that you must allow you the time that is needed to release and allow it through your nervous system, and out of your memory banks. Your pain is basically traveling out of you, and as it moves it triggers the warning system in your brain that tells your body to prepare for a big problem.

As you release this pain, you will become very sensitive and perhaps overwhelmed. This is why I tell you to leave your current situation if it is not the most loving and caring. Most of you will re-create a similar situation unless you have unloaded most of your *magnetic* debris. You are often unconscious of what you carry and this is how you are allowed to *see* what you carry. This reflection theory was actually meant to be a gift, until you began to judge what you saw reflected back to you as bad. Then you began to hate your own reflections instead of changing your stance so you could reflect a different position.

When you begin to clear your pain, you will release in various ways and anger will move in you. You will get upset over the least little thing, and I am asking you now to stay calm. You may yell and scream all you want, but this pain must come up and out, so you do not kill this particular body with it. If you do not wish to clear your pain you will not need to be concerned by this particular writing.

As you begin to release this pain I do wish you peace. Try to focus on the fact that you are simply releasing, and do not yell at others. I say this not out of judgment, but to keep things calm. Once you begin to scream your pain at others, you may create greater confusion and pain for yourself. It is best to wait it out and be as careful and kind with yourself as possible. After all, it is your pain and you created it in the first place, by judging you as not good for something that occurred. Now is a time to accept you and release judgment in order to release pain.

As you go into your pain you may find that you wish to tell everyone what you really think of them. This too could create bigger problems for you, as you would simply be speaking *from* your pain and not from truth. As this pain leaves, you will feel great relief and at times you will wish to sing and dance. This singing and dancing part is toward the end when you begin to re-light your own source of joy. I want you to know that this pain is not all bad. Some of it is not even real. Some pain was created out of something that you only thought occurred.

Have you ever been listening to a conversation and *thought* you heard someone speak poorly regarding you and your behavior? Maybe this conversation was between your parents, and you, as a small child, *thought* they were upset with you or perhaps no longer wanted you. So you overhear this conversation and you feel like you should run away from home only you are afraid to. So now you are stuck where you *believe* you are not wanted by your parents, and you are afraid to leave because you are too small to be out on your own.

You now have this programmed into your little brain; "My parents are upset with me and do not want me." Tomorrow when you wake up you will probably forget all about it, because a child learns to shut off what hurts and keep what feels good. So, next day you are yourself again, with no thought of running away. You may even find out later that your parents were actually talking about their new dog that they are having problems training, and wondering if he (or she) is worth keeping. So you heard "he" (or "she") and, of course, you thought it was you they were discussing.

Now we have this problem concerning your original "thought" and the pain connected to it. You shut it off so you would not have to feel pain and you (somewhere inside) believe your parents want to get rid of you. So, where is this thought? How do we access it to "release" the stored pain behind the judgment of "I am bad, they want to be rid of me?" It is all stored *within* you. Every bit of pain from every lifetime you have lived has unseen pain. I suggest that if your pain is great you shut yourself off from others until you can be "free" enough to deal with relationships. You are not wrong to leave, you are not wrong to shut yourself in a room. You are saving your life and this is good!

I now wish to discuss your health. As you begin to release anger and, of course, your pain that created your anger, you will begin to be ill, or tired, or worn down. You may develop colds or even flu symptoms. This is due to the fact that all disease in the body is caused by how you *feel.* And if how you feel is sad or hurt it will reflect in your body.

So, as you begin to erase your pain you may re-create the disease or diseases that went with your pain. These diseases may come up all at once or one at a time, depending upon how you release your illness. All pain is disease and all disease is some sort of connected pain.

When it comes to disorders this too is pain, be it an eating disorder or a bodily function disorder. If you have certain body parts misplaced, it is a good idea to look at why you created this disorder. Your body will function perfectly if you are in harmony. One of the problems we have at this time is denial. Denial is so strong that you may not be aware that you have pain. You will find that if you have strong denial you may not feel your own pain. You may have shut your pain off so you do not have to deal with, or listen to it. If this is the case, you have also shut off your feelings, so you do not have to deal with these as well.

For those of you who have shut-off, you will find it more difficult to get in touch with your own true identity. You may have to go very deep in you before you *feel*. Feeling is not bad. So do not be afraid to feel. If, however, you have stuffed and buried your feelings you may have to dig very deep to uncover who you are.

You are not so much a product of your environment as you are a product of how you respond to your environment. You are not meant to be in pain, you are meant to be in light, love and joy. Once we get you straightened out and headed in this direction, you will see the light and begin to receive your gifts more readily. If you face the light you cannot help but see the light. Many of you are not in a position to see the light and we must *move* you into your pain so you may be moved into your joy.

Once you discover that you will not die while reliving your pain, you will know that it is safe to look at all parts of you. You are not so frail that you cannot take a good look at yourself and all that you have created for yourself. The *desire* to look within will bring about the needed results. As you desire to heal yourself you will begin to see ways to do so. After all, you are reading this book and something guided you to it. It is no coincidence that you chose it or were given it.

If you have not done so before, now I wish to recommend the use of enema as a healing tool. It is a most enjoyable way to discharge all pain and disease from your body. It is recommended throughout this series of books and you may wish to recommend it to yourself, as your way of dealing with your blocked off parts. Open up by letting the darkness out of you. This is my way to teach you to heal at this particular time. Times may change and with them techniques will change. For now, I have done what I can to show you a simple, effective, inexpensive, life-saving way to heal yourself.

You have read in this series how Liane has used this technique and how she has fared. It is not yet certain if she will continue to write God's books or if she will move on to other ways of doing God's work. It is certain that she has grown tremendously and her perception has shifted dramatically. She has begun to see the light without the use of external support.

You see, Liane was held in place in order to begin this work for God. She was put in a position where she could feel trust and faith in order to move her into her own trust and faith. She found a great joy in everyday living and was always with God and speaking with God. In this state she channeled my first three books. After those first three books, we allowed Liane to begin to descend into her pain, loneliness, fear, hatred and anger. She had a very good support system as she went down to these lower vibrations, but she still felt all alone and hurt.

Now she is coming back up, to see the light from her own knowledge of who she is. Her efforts to go within worked and she uncovered her deep, dark secret and looked at her experience and how she judged herself as well as others. Now she stands in the light of day with full knowledge of who she is, not only knowledge of this life and her childhood, but also knowledge of past life and its pain and judgments.

So she has come full circle and it took a very short time even by your standards. Now she may choose her next path and walk into her future free of programming, and debris, and all that baggage she was carrying. That baggage weighs you down and wears you out. Put down your baggage and walk out into the light "free" of your perceptions. Know who you are and ask to be shown how you are. You will not get back to God by ignoring God. God is in you. You are in God. Know you and you know God!

᪴

*W*hen you begin to love again you will know joy. Joy will come from not caring if you are losing or winning, because you are not here to win or lose. You are here to love! There really is no other reason to be here. It is love that is being born and the love that is being born is finding its way into you.

You will find that you no longer need to be right, or on top, or better than anyone. You will only want to give and you will have come to know that all giving is receiving. You are on your way to healing when you can do for you what you do for others. When you can love you, and need you, and want you, and even dress up for you, you will be romancing you. Buy you flowers and show you and tell you how beautiful you are. You are your own romantic date and you must learn to appreciate all of you.

You are now at the crossroads where you will decide if you are to be love or fear. You may continue to fear or you may ask to love. Ask to love you and ask often. It is no longer appropriate to ask God to send you someone to love. I have sent you someone to love and that someone is you. Why is this not enough for you? Do you need more of you or less of you? Are you happy with this you or are you upset that you got stuck with you?

You may change, you know? You may become absolutely anything you wish to be. You may be happy or sad, love or fear, joy or pain. You may even be peace or war. What is your choice... your pleasure? It is all for you, you know? You create it and design it and now it is time to give up your dysfunctional behavior so you might "see the gift" in all creation.

The secret is this, "there is no right way or wrong way." There only "is," and what "is" is what you get. You get what you believe you deserve, and if you do not believe you deserve you will throw away gold, because to you it looks like a dirty, misshapen, piece of rock. Ah! But to the dreamer and lover it is pure gold even when it is not. So who is the most nuts? The one who loves everything or the one who loves nothing because he is afraid he is being tricked?

This is how your fear and your pain has tricked you and paralyzed you. It said, "Do not trust or you get hurt real bad!" And now I am telling you to trust again. Give yourself one more chance to prove that you will not hurt yourself again. Give yourself one more chance to prove that *you* can create beauty and love and joy of living. Give yourself one more chance to prove you are God and you do not make mistakes. Give yourself one more chance to know that you are love, and give yourself one more chance to become love.

It all happened for a reason you know? You didn't blindly stumble into this life or that life and screw up. There are no mistakes. You know exactly what you are doing and why. Now is the time to trust you, to love you and to take you by the hand and congratulate you for making it this far and doing such a fine job.

❧

*B*efore you know it you will be learning how to overcome your programming. You will begin to see how you re-create the exact situation over and over in your life and how to change that situation into a positive one. You may find that you no longer wish to be frail and weak and pushed around by others. This is the victim role. Or you may find that you no longer wish to be pushy and loud and run people away from you. This, of course, is the position of the predator.

You have been playing both roles for a very long time and now I wish you to come into balance. I know it is not so much that you do not wish to balance, as it is you not quite knowing how to balance. This is why I write through Liane. I wish to heal Liane and, in the process, if I should help one or two more.... Great!

It is not so much out of love that I heal; it is because I cannot inhabit Liane's body and share space with darkness and illness. It just does not work and something must go. Light turns on – dark disappears. It is not possible to have darkness and light at the same moment. You are one or the other and since Liane was overloaded with her share of dark energy, I had to make some adjustments so God could move into her otherwise inhabited form.

She is not so much darkness now as she once was. I was able to shine light on her dark areas and she was able to look directly at her pain and grief. She saw and now she does not fear discovering her own truth; the truth that she had sex as a child and judged herself as a villain. You have a great deal of pain attached to these types of situations and I wish you to outgrow this pain and become "bigger" than the darkness it carries.

Once you learn how to go into your pain, you will know how to be light. Light will *allow* you to face your pain and see the truth of the entire situation. The truth for Liane is that she was held down and forced to have sex. She honored the wishes of an adult and did not run or fight. She did not trust that this person could actually harm her and so she took on the *judgment* that she must be the one at fault. She is not at fault and she is now aware that neither is he. She held her pain and her secret for so long that she became ill and nearly killed herself from stress.

The stress is gone and Liane is free of her judgment *against* herself. She no longer believes she is a bad girl, or person, and she is now "free" to love her self. She is not so much like you as she is you. You are each connected to one another and what affects one affects the whole. So in cleaning out one cell in my body and making room for light I can literally affect millions.

This is the gift. It is for those who ask to be healed and for those who are ready to listen. For if you do not hear what I say, how can you possibly know what has been given to you in the form of information? You will find that often you do not listen, because you believe you already know best. You have taken your stance and you know that what you have chosen to believe is the truth, and someone else's *position* is just their idea of what is going on. This may be, but I do wish you would learn to look at all perspectives, not just yours and theirs, but all perspectives.

It will allow you to become a totally new person with *expanded* vision. See it all! See it from every angle and allow it to be valid for whichever position it is chosen to support. The validity of truth is in the seeing, and the seeing is simply in the stance or position you can see from.

Liane has an old friend who once told her to see truth as a giant tree that the entire world could stand around. From point "A" you could see the leaves and birds but from point "C" you could not, you could only see some wood rot and pitch. Does point "A" have more validity than "C?" I think not. It is all in where you stand, and if you can learn to stand *above* any situation you will see not only two sides to every situation, you will see all sides.

Now, when you begin to see all sides you begin to defend no one and nothing. There is really no reason to, because there is no predator and no victim. There are only dramas being acted out. So from this perspective, you do not wish to save Liane from sexual abuse as she *chose* sexual abuse to grow and rise *above* a situation.

So; what do you do now? Whatever will you do on earth when you no longer have this good guy/bad guy game you play? Life may become very boring for you and you may just have to resort to *peace*. Could it be that you will play this game until the truth comes out and then you will have to find another game to occupy your time? You will learn to rise up and leave the game table when you have learned that judgment can only be used in situations of good guy/bad guy. Without the *belief* in good or bad, or good vs. evil, there is no game and judgment leaves as it is no longer applicable from a higher point of view.

***

*W*hen you begin to see how you have created all that you currently see, you will know that it is not so big a mistake as it is a mess of confusion. Once you come out of your confusion you will know that you no longer have pain. This confusion causes you to scramble around to resolve your current situation when, in actuality, you are creating the very situation you justify needs resolving.

This is your big push me/pull me. You are what you do not wish to be. You are not only the effect, you are the cause. You are not only the created experience; you are the creator of your experiences. You are not only the one who made it all happen; you are the one who tries to stop it from happening.

So; how do you get control over you? How do you begin to know that you are God and allow yourself the freedom to create as God? Or how do you live and not die? How do you create from only love with no fear that what you create may be wrong? How is it that you do not wish to be God and why do you not wish to be responsible for what you yourself have created? How long will it take to defuse this entire situation and how often will you hurt you in order to show you that you have pain?

Well, if we can all sit down and stop yelling and screaming for God to intervene, and if you will all be calm I will help. Stay calm. Be peaceful and quiet as much as you can. Stay as quiet as you can without creating more of your "created pain." Stop being so adamant about solving and fixing everyone else's problems. Begin to focus solely on you. Stay out of gunfire! There are many who are going-off right now and, if someone is exploding, stand back and keep your distance from the flying debris. Focus on inner peace and tranquility until I can get you to a place of awareness. Stop struggling and begin to go within. You have expanded and taken-on enough. Now I want you to take-off, let-go-of, and release.

This entire situation has been blown out of proportion and I wish you all to stop yelling and screaming and fighting with one another. Simply stop and refuse to rebuke or rebuttal. This is your God given right. When someone pushes at you to stir things up "let it go." Do not get involved and do not play the argument or war game with them. You have gotten to the point that you create friction to expand and excite yourselves. Do not get involved. Do not get riled up. Stay calm. Peace and inner awareness will come from calm not from action. Stay in one place long enough to feel who you are.

You are not love and light at this time. You are fear and darkness at its biggest. You will become love and light by knowing that *you are the one who is creating everything you are looking at.* If you see it, it is yours. If you do not see it, you did not give it any power and you do not own it. You may easily know what you have contributed to, it is in your line of vision and you know of it. If you do not know of it, it is not yours.

You can also know that you are seeing a reality and be unaware that you do. You may view a position and not give yourself information regarding your own viewpoint. I will give you an example. My pen believed kindness to be most important and judged ill will or unkindness. This created conflict for her as she believed part of kindness to be "loving all who came to her." So if she decided they had ill will or unkind thoughts toward her, she went into *denial* in order to allow them to be what she considered kind. So now we have her intuition saying this is what is going on here and her denial saying, "No, this is a kind person, I must be wrong."

After her denial became so big that she could no longer judge for herself how someone behaved, she began to simply judge herself for everything she perceived to be unkind. This, of course, creates great confusion for her and she takes on the responsibility of having unkind thoughts, when in actuality she is sensing what is sometimes being projected at her, not from her. This may or may not be a reflection. In a mirror reflection you see what you are. Unkind thoughts are showing her that she carries unkind thoughts toward herself that do not belong to her.

She may see unkind thoughts as a way of killing off parts of herself which she just cannot accept, or she may see unkind thoughts as simply being bad, therefore she gets to be the bad girl she believes herself to be. In this way she reinforces her own reality or belief that she is bad and she is the one to blame in all situations of unkind behavior.

You are either unloading or loading and I wish you to stop long enough to uncover your behavior and find out if you are truly playing the victim or if you are covering your true role which is bad guy. Many of you who play the bad guy or believe you are the bad guy are playing the victim in order to "feed your need" to be punished. Stop punishing and allow you to rest.

≈‖≈

As long as you continue to be spirit in matter, you will continue to be overwhelmed by matter. Once you learn that you are spirit in charge of matter, you will see how you do not need to answer to compulsive body behavior.

It is a matter of learning who you are and being who you are. It is a matter of being free, as spirit is meant to be free. It is a matter of being spirit now and not waiting to die to become spirit. It is a matter of being "free" now and not feeling trapped. You *are* spirit; you do not belong to a spirit. You are body; you do not belong to a body. You are free to choose how you will exist. You are free to decide how you will respond. The only prison you see is one of your own creation. You have created your own hell and it is time to rise up into heaven.

You are not so much a prisoner of body as you are of mind. Your mind is in control and it has lost its grip on reality. It has viewed so many realities that it believes strongly it has *become* one of them. It has not; it is only programming itself to accept this or that regarding who you are. You are not the one who believes in you. You believe what your mind tells you and what your mind tells you is that you are limited. You are not. You are unlimited and you are free to be who and what you are.

When you begin to know how you respond to your own mind, you will be far ahead of this game that you play with yourself. You are not so much out of control as you are out of touch with reality. You no longer *view* the truth, you now view a lie. The lie tells you to not trust and to not believe in yourself. Your truth will tell you "you are God" and to trust yourself. Your lie will tell you that "you do not know what you are doing," so you must never trust yourself and let yourself get ahead of your mind. You keep you in check at all times for fear you will lose control, but it is your mind that is afraid of losing its control over you.

You follow your mind like it is God and it is not your God. Let go of who you believe you are and begin to be who you know you are. You are not so much out of control as you are in your mind. Get out of your mind. Learn to see from all perspectives and learn to *allow* absolutely everything to be a gift!

I will now discuss your right to life. You each have a right to live and to experience life in whatever fashion works for you. You are not so much afraid to live as you are afraid to live for you. You are afraid to be who you are and you are afraid to be wrong. You spend your entire life trying to do the right thing or be right. Now is the time to be you.

Do not allow you to become so afraid of making choices that you give your choices away to another. When you give your choices away to another you are giving your power to that person. Do not be so alone and afraid that you give you away. You are not only worthy you are God. God is not in the habit of bowing down to others for permission to live. Most of what you know, you have forgotten and when you remember what you have forgotten, you will no longer fear living for yourself.

As you go about your daily lives, I wish you to remember that you are in every situation you are in for a

Loving Light, Book 11

very good reason. Learn to accept your situations and to
know you are learning to grow and evolve. If you are not
happy in a situation or it does not feel good, then I suggest
you let go of this situation. Sometimes the lesson is just
that simple.

Now; there is a very big difference between getting
what you want and getting your needs met. Often you get
what you want, but after you do, you get upset because this
thing, or situation, is not fulfilling your needs as you
thought. This is the price you pay for chasing after your
outside world in order to feed your inner hunger. Your
inner hunger can only be supplied and nourished by you.
You are the one who can nourish and love you.

When you begin to know that everyone and
everything outside of you is a *reflection* of what is *in* you, you
will have an easier time figuring out what situation you are
in and why. It is okay to leave the situation and it is okay to
stay. It is up to you, and to run is not wrong, and to hide is
not wrong, and to stay and fight is not wrong. One may be
more draining than the other, but sometimes, in draining
one's energy in battle, one *learns* that it is no fun to fight.
So, how can fighting be bad if one learns and grows from
it?

When you begin to know who you are you will
begin to know that you are loved and you are being guided
back into your own love. You are not being guided into
someone else's love; you are being guided into your own
love. As you learn to love yourself, you will learn to know
who you are and how you are creating only the best for
yourself. *Know the self*, this is most important in your

survival and your growth. Wisdom is at a premium and the greater knowledge you have concerning your behavior and programming the greater chance of breaking through it to get to you; the real you.

When you begin to find out who you are, you may have a very difficult time being around people, accepting people and liking people. This is due to the fact that you do not like nor accept your own self. So, of course, when these feelings come up for you this is all you can see. You will find something wrong with everything, only because you are looking at a direct reflection of your own self and, to you, you are awful and icky.

So, does your world seem to be awful and icky with everything wrong, or is it beautiful and full of love? This is the time to be honest. No one is here but you and I, and you and I already know the truth. You are not so afraid to be honest as you are afraid of being rejected for being honest, so many of you pretend to be loving when you do not *feel* loving and you pretend to be good when you do not feel good. It is all you learning to accept all parts of you even if you have to pretend you do.

When you truly love and are love, you will no longer feel the need to pretend. You will feel honesty and you will feel truth and you will not be ashamed of your truth and the telling of it. It is not meant to be pushed at others and it is not meant to be buried under shame and self denial. It is meant to *be* part of you and you may share it or not share it. It is not as if in the sharing of your truth, you change someone else's life or even affect their life. You may affect your own life in the sharing of your truth and another may affect his or her own life by receiving that truth, but it is impossible for you to be the cause of someone else's evolution. You do not own one another and you do not have the ability to raise another in consciousness.

Yes! You have the ability to raise your own level of consciousness, but those of you who believe you are saving others, or raising them up by your actions, are only feeding your own *need* to feel good about yourself and what you do. You do not take credit for another's learning or training. Information given is simply that. It is given. If it is received then it is the cause of the receiver not the giver. Do not believe that you are so noble as to teach the world your truth and raise it up. There is one way to raise up the world and that way is to raise you, because you are the world and the world is you.

So, keep it at home and *in* you. You are not the effect if you do not wish to be. You are the cause. You do not *need* to feed off of others by telling them how to live and then reassuring yourself that you have done this wonderful thing. You did nothing more than put some words into the air. They will choose if these words fit their needs to heal and they will choose if they *receive* your words.

If you do not offend others by teaching them, how can you possibly offend them by not teaching them? Stop teaching and begin to learn. When you play the teacher you play the controller or one in power. Start learning and growing, and give away your intelligent attitude and become a student. You have a great deal to learn regarding who you are and how you control your life and others in order to feel safe and on top of every situation.

God is not safe and on top. God is love. Nothing else is even here. When you get this you will know what it is to be *all*, not on top, not smarter than, just everything.

❧

I will now tell you how you will reach God. God is in you and you will reach into God by reaching into you. You will find God as you find you, and you will discover God as you discover you. You may find that you no longer wish to be God and that you wish to hide your shame and your denial of God.

As you begin to grow in awareness and enlightenment, you begin to see how you are all that exists here. You will come to a place of enlightenment that is most appropriate for learning. When you come to this place and you begin to learn, you will have anxiety about who you are. Once you give up knowing who you think you are and begin to ask, "Okay, who am I and what am I?" you will begin to receive your answers and you will learn to let go of your old identity. You are now learning to create an entirely new you just by telling yourself to change.

As you begin to change, you will take on many new roles in order to see how you wish to be. You may become tougher or softer. You may become louder or quieter. You may become beautiful or ugly. It is all a matter of choice.

As you *choose* how you will appear to yourself and to others, you will find that you are acting different from how you would normally act. This is due to you *becoming* the new you. You are changing and growing and re-creating a new personality based on new insight and greater truth.

Those of you who get louder are simply balancing the issues you have regarding being quiet and unobtrusive. Those who become quiet are learning to balance their issues regarding noise and loud behavior. I want you to remember that there are no wrong choices and if you choose to be loud you will find those who share this choice with you. Do not impose your behavior on another and do not expect a quiet person to stick around. You will find that those who choose quiet and calm will draw together in quiet and calm. They too will not wish to judge quiet or loud. They too are learning to balance and will find it uncomfortable to be around those who choose loud and obtrusive behavior.

Now; when you choose ugly or beautiful you are simply choosing a mask. This is your choice of a costume and if you always see yourself as ugly you will begin to project ugly outward to others. This is how you create. If you see beauty, you project beauty out to others. When you begin to see how all of this works you will see how you are not being punished by God, you have simply chosen a role to play.

You will learn that you do not become God simply by acting like you have all the answers. You actually must let go of all the answers to be God. God carries nothing, not even answers. As you begin to see how you are losing parts of you and becoming less of what you are, you will see how you are not only afraid to be you, you are upset that you must become you. You are upset with God that you do not play a better role, or carry a different identity and so God is showing you how you are the one who chose to be this you, and the good news is you can totally change whatever part you do not like.

Do not kill you out of dissatisfaction toward who and what you are. You have always died in order to return and get a fresh start with a new body. I am trying to show you how this you is perfect and it is only *your* judgment of you that creates any dislike or problem in your life. If you do not like who you are, change. Do not charge others with non-acceptance of you just as you are. It is you who do not accept you just as you are.

When you find that you are simply judging and creating all your own problems you will be relieved, because now you will know that you may change you by dropping the judgment you hold against you. So; what did you do to create judgment and how did you cause your own pain or dislike of self? You are in this class to learn and I wish you to learn why you aren't happy and how you are hating you, and in doing so you will let go of hatred and your body will begin to heal. It is not an impossible task to heal. It only takes time and wanting or desiring health and light. It does not take a great mind and it is often very simple and a step-by-step process.

Take the first step now. Go look in your mirror and say, "I take full responsibility for myself and I will learn to heal myself." Then give yourself a great big hug and walk out into the light, and know that you just began the process of turning you around. You just began the process by which you will grow in love of self. The only love there is, is self-love. It is a light and it cannot be given away to another. No one can ever take your love from you and run. It is yours forever and you are the only one who can feel it, as it is you.

When you come together with another and you begin to pin your hopes and dreams on them, you are not loving them you are simply handing your hopes and dreams over to them, in hopes they will create them for you. You are responsible for creating for you and if you feel abandoned by others it may be that you expected them to take care of your reality and they, of course, have their own and felt quite overburdened carrying yours too.

You must take full responsibility for all that you create. This is not a time to be handing what you want over to others. Keep you for you and learn to love you. You will not fall apart if you stand alone with only you. You are God and if you stand alone you stand as God. God does not crave nor seek comfort for his pain from others. To seek comfort is taught to you in order to create dependency on others. You fill you with your own good and all the others will simply follow suit. Then we will have an entire army of gods and we will not fight nor will we march, we will simply shine!

As far as I can see, you have no problem finding ways to love someone else. Now I want you to learn to love you and find ways to love you. You are so ready to give yourselves over to others for companionship, or for fear of lack of security. The minute you are afraid you reach out to someone. This is how you are so *attached* to so many people and so many things.

I want you to reach in not out. When you hurt go *in* to you. When you are lonely go *in* to you. When you are afraid go *in* to you. You will learn to trust you by counting solely on you. You will learn that you create what you create in order to care for you. If you get a good raise at work it is because you created it, not because you have a wonderful, sensitive boss. Your boss is doing what is best for him which seems to be "keeping you happy." If he were not so interested in his own care and place in life he would not care whether you received or not.

If you do not wish to owe your life to others stop pretending that others *create* your life for you. Take the credit and take responsibility for what is yours. Some of you go too far out on a limb and begin to claim credit for all that you believe you do for others, and this too is you taking care of you. You do what makes you feel good about yourself and no one owes anyone else. No one ever gives, as you can only give to the self and no one ever receives from another, as you are responsible for what *you* have just given to you.

Stop owing and stop buying. You cannot create your own heaven on earth if you are so caught up in who created what for you. You created it all and you are responsible for *everything* that occurs in your life. You are not a pawn, you are not a king. When someone infers that you owe them because they have been very good to you, I wish you to know that they gave what they gave in order to get what they wanted. Maybe what they wanted was to be part of your world or maybe what they wanted was to attach to you. It could also be that what they wanted was to feel better about themselves by being the giver or caretaker.

Most often in these cases it is a matter of trade-off. What the person who is playing "giver" is really doing is finding someone to lord over. When you are very insecure you may give to others in order to get them in your camp, so to speak, or on your side. You all do this. You play this game of giving and receiving and it is ridiculous because you cannot give or receive to anyone but you.

So, each time you feel so upset about how much you did for someone and how little they gave in return, I wish you to remember that you had your own reasons for what you did and I want you to begin to look closely at your reasons. You did not give anything away as it is impossible to give to anyone but you. So look at what you received in this situation that you created for you.

*W*hen you begin to know love you will begin to understand that you do not love another and love has nothing to do with feelings. Love is. It is not something you either experience or do not experience. You are love and love will not and cannot leave you. As you begin to understand how love always is and is not something you strive for, you will know that you are complete and whole just as you are.

You need never search for love, as love is not lost. Love is you! You *are* love! You are that essence that is all life forms and all beingness. You are complete and everlasting and even infinite love. You have no depth as there are no boundaries. When you learn to *unlearn* everything you have been taught here you will be *free* to see love. You are not so much blind as you are in the dark, and the darkness is moving to make room for the dawning of light. Light will become the center of this creation and light will allow all to see how there is nothing to fear. Light is this thing you call love. Love is the essence of you.

You do not need to search for light. You do not need to search for love. You are simply taking off what you have put on in an attempt to block out what you are. You wished to sleep so you blocked out light to allow you to doze. Now we are pulling back the drapes to show you that you are all there is.

You want so desperately to find someone to love and the truth is that you are the someone you are searching so desperately to find. You are your own twin soul. You are the other half of you. You will walk hand-in-hand with you as you return to your wholeness. You are no longer separated or split. You are coming together with your own self; your own other half.

As you begin to become more of you, you will draw those who are more of you. Your reflections will become greater or more magnified until they actually begin to feel like you. You may get confused and think you are some part of them, when in actuality, you are all of them. You are the creator, so as you create greater light, you create greater reflections with greater detail or clarity. You may begin to see immediately how you are creating this or that reflection or you may begin to "read" that reflection with certain clarity. This is when you are getting very clear on you. You cannot see another clearly without first *seeing* you. You are projecting this image, so you can only read it clearly if you recognize it as your reflection.

Now; when you begin to see such a close reflection you may wish to "reach out" to this reflection because you feel it's pain. Please remember that it is your reflection you wish to help or reach out to and it is your reflected pain. When you reach this level of reflected composure, you must not get involved with fixing or helping your reflection. Go to the source of this reflection, which is you, and help or fix you. Do not put your energy out and into a reflection when you can put your energy right *in* you where it already lives. Heal you and you heal the world. It is so simple. Everything is so simple. What reflections will you draw when you are healed and on your way to "heaven on earth?" Will you not draw like reflections? Of course you will, as you can only draw what you contain.

Let it all go and heal you. Let the pain of the world leave your body and you will know only joy. In this joy, you will draw reflections of joy. If you could be God for one day you could see how perfect this all is. You are not in a position to be God only because of the drawn curtains. We will raise the shade, and open the drapes, and allow only light to shine when we have you empty. Empty your tank. Empty your head and allow space to fill you. Allow all the garbage you have been fed, both figuratively and mentally, to leave you. You are not what you believe and now we must teach you how you are nothing.

The layers of programming are simply the belief system that you created. Now we are going to erase it and erase you; the "you" you thought you were. You are no longer this you, as this you is simply a mass of beliefs and judgments and thoughts about how it should be. To be love there are no rules and no "should be's." There is only you, shining bright under a load of garbage. It will take time to dig through and throw out this garbage, but it will feel so good when it is gone and you are stripped bare. I know you are afraid to have any more taken from you, but you will find this strip-down rather lightening as well as enlightening. It is only a short time now. We are well on our way.

I will always allow you freedom to choose. You are the one who decides how you will live and how you will die. You will choose if you will ascend to a new level or if you will continue with your current patterns. You are not so much learning to choose as you are learning that you have a choice. You are the one who must decide whether you are rich or poor, king or pauper, soldier or priest. You decide how you will play your role and even how this role will or will not affect you.

You must be the one to decide how you will rise or not rise. You must be the one to choose whether you leave the unnecessary garbage behind or whether you wish to cling to it. You are going or you are staying. This choice is totally up to you and has no credence or bearing on you as God, because with or without conscious awareness of the fact... you are God!

As you begin to consider how long you stay and how fast you can go, you may determine that a change in position might do you a world of good; maybe even get you unstuck from some of the garbage that has begun to take over. When you make your choice I will be here to assist you, as I am going nowhere and I have always been a big part of you. You will find that as you learn to be more of you, you are actually becoming more of me. We are integrating and becoming whole.

For those who do not believe you are God, you will wish to know that it does not matter. You will learn in due time the truth of all "matter" and you will no longer believe yourself to be so alone. You will find that you are not only not alone you *are* everyone and everything. You created all of creation and you laid down to rest and forgot to wake up. Now you don't know who you are, let alone recognize the truth of "matter" when it is presented to you.

You are trying so hard to figure out how to survive in all of this matter that you will not *receive* the simplest explanations for it. You are in a position to learn how you did this and you are in a position to change everything you wish to change. You need not struggle and you need not suffer. You may change and see how not to suffer. You may change and see how not to struggle. Do you wish to change, or do you wish to continue to judge and not accept that those reflected images are just that? They are reflected images of you.

So; let go of your need to change the image and get down to the job of changing you. Let go of your garbage and stop collecting more. You are like a street person who huddles with all of his or her bags in a cart and you won't relinquish even one for fear you might lose something you need. You do not *need* fear and pain. We are taking your bags away now and you may scream and feel you are losing, but try to remember that it is only matter. It is garbage in a bag that you have carried since childhood and you even brought some of this old rotten stuff in with you from past lives.

It is not you. This garbage is stuck to you and you cling to it for security. I will tell you how we will do this. I will tug gently at your bags of garbage, and that way you will know that this area of you is ready to let go and let

God have control. When you feel the tug it may upset you and you may get afraid that you are losing. Don't be afraid. Let it all go so that you will be free of that one bag. The next time, I will tug at another bag that is unnecessary for you to carry. You may think, "Oh no, I'm losing everything. Don't I get to keep anything?" And as you have this thought, I want you to remember, "Oh yes, God said he was going to tug at the unnecessary garbage. This must be his way of tugging." Then, of course, you will feel safe in releasing your grip, as you will know that I am working with you and it is all for a very good reason!

For such a long time you have been developing. And what you are developing into is changing. You are now becoming more of what you are by becoming less of who you think you are. As you become less of who you think you are, you actually deflate your ego so he can rest. Ego has had a very hard time keeping up with the demand for perfection and co-operation and flat out hope for something better in life. Ego is the one who must become active and 'charge' you in order to deliver your goods. Ego is the one who stands by and registers hurts and insensitivities done to you by others. Ego is your greatest defense, and ego is your most open wound.

You will find that as you begin to come into

balance your ego will panic. He is losing his identity and is no longer big shot or king on the mount. When your ego begins to lose control you may feel a little deflated, or let down, or not as good as you thought you were. You are losing a position, a stance, an idea that says, "This is how I see myself."

Do not expect to find the ego happy about letting go of your current position. He most enjoys being the one with all the answers, or top dog in the pack. As your ego deflates, he is going to find that small is not bad and to be you is just as wonderful as trying to put on airs. As your ego comes back into balance you will find that you are not only learning to let go of who you think you are, you are also letting go of your identity as the smart one with the answer for everyone. Or maybe your identity is the helpful one who doles out answers for those in trouble. This could be your job title or your personality. As you know many job titles offer this ability to you.

So, as you get off your high horse and begin to say, "I don't know, I'm just a student myself," you begin to allow you to be the same as, and not smarter than, everyone else. Now we all get to be equal. Okay, so you have a degree in math or psychology, so what? Maybe that actually makes you a little denser than the next person, because now you have to unlearn all the positionality that you have been taught. Now you have more learning to unlearn. So who is smarter and who knows more, the guy with less programming or the guy with more programming? Just a thought!

So, when your identity begins to slip away and you

begin to feel like you are losing and becoming a nobody, you are actually becoming more of who and what you really are, which is less than what you think you are. Trust me on this one; go for less it will feel better.

❧

*A*s you begin to recover from losing, you will see how you have not lost and you are now calm. You are working up to becoming your own source and as you do so you are letting go of your needs. Your needs are based on your fears and without fear there is no need. Say you fear not having food, for you have been taught that without food you starve to death. Your *need* for food is now based on your fear of death.

This is also how you see each and every situation where you need something. You need a mate so you will no longer feel alone. Your fear of being alone brings you to this need. You need money so you will not be living in the streets. Your need for money comes from fear of not having a shelter to provide safety in a storm. Your fear of being unsafe brings on the need for shelter.

So; we have three basic needs or fears; shelter, food, love. Which do you fear the most? Are you most afraid of being unloved and alone, or are you most afraid of being homeless and without a place to sleep? How about hunger? Does hunger ever enter your mind? Have you gone without food and been afraid of not having the nourishment you require? Yes. Some of you have. Some of you have been starved to death and are so afraid of doing so again that you will do anything to stay warm and fed.

You have been returning and re-creating the same scenario over and over again since the beginning of time. It's time to wake up and stop pretending that you fear death or any other discomfort. You are not afraid of dying, because you know you go on and you do not end. Only this part of you believes in death, and this part of you is very small and uninformed.

As you begin to move through the layers that have created life as you now know it, you will find that life is based on a lie and a fear. Life, as you now know it, is based on the veil theory. This is that you must continue to hide behind the veil and play frail and innocent of any past knowledge of what you are really doing here. The veil is the secret that you are hiding. You are pretending to be the victim of this game in order to continue playing this game.

Now; when I tell you repeatedly that you will have it all when you return to God, you will have all of you which is everything that is. How can you not have part of you when you are creator and you are creation? When you feel like you are having everything taken from you, you are actually gaining the rest of you. You are actually growing in you. You are expanding by letting go. You are becoming more of your own true identity by letting go of this false identity that you carry.

You are not so much out of balance with God as you are out of character. You stepped out of identity and now you must return to owning your true identity. Your true identity will not harm you. It is not painful to be God. It is not lonely to be God. It is not harmful to be God. It is love and joy and white light. It is brightness and peace like you have not experienced since you left. You have forgotten how nice it can be. You have traveled into your creations and taken on so much density and pain that now you have no memory of "light" and non-pain.

You have lived with so much pain that you literally crave pain. It makes you feel alive. When you feel emotional pain, you register a sense of attunement with your body and your emotions. You get all sad and hurt and you pout, because it "feels" like something and you are so grateful to "feel" so you won't think you have gone dead emotionally. It is not the hurt that you crave so much as it is the charge. The charge is the "zing" we discussed earlier. This "zing" gets you all riled up and boy do you feel alive and you come out fighting, or running, whichever is your *habit*.

You are all habitual and you all crave the "zing" and you will re-create it in your life as often as necessary to make you "feel" alive. Only now we must create a bigger "zing" with greater charge because this density that you carry is getting thicker and it takes a greater charge to get through it to you. So you create greater *charges* in your life just to open your eyes and make you know that you exist.

I wish you to learn to live without these charges, without the stimulus that provokes your emotions into a frenzied state. Can you live without pain? Can you let go of pain? You will need to let go of your needs in order to let

5125555555555555555

go of pain. If you can let go of your needs you can live pain-free. The needs create the "belief" in pain. "If the needs go unmet there will be a problem, there will be a big hurt," this is the belief I wish you to let go of. There will be no big hurt. God is God, and God has no needs nor does God fear losing. Let it all go. Do not fear dying and do not fear losing. Let it be. It is okay to die and it is okay to have nothing. It is also okay to have no one.

Now; this writing will turn you off and will not appeal to you if you are not sincere in your effort to "let go and let God." Once you've totally let go, you no longer *hold* to you, and your hands and mind are free to receive what Liane calls the good stuff. Let go of everything you now believe and become a blank receptor. It is not long after you become blank that you begin to receive.

When you become so sure of yourself that you no longer mistrust who you are, you will have the determination to rise even higher. You will know that you are creating it all and you will know that you are creating what is best for you. As you begin to rise above confusion and self defeat, you will see how you are not only the creator, you are love. Your love will begin to show through.

This is when you begin to wonder just how you ever hid it from you in the first place. It takes a great deal of determination to block out the light. It takes all sorts of energy and effort to play down the fact that you are who you are. It is no simple matter to wake up and it is no simple matter to sleep. Either case has its meaning and purpose. You went to sleep to block out the light and you are waking up to let in the light. You rested and you "fell" into a very deep subconscious sleep, and now you are rousing and stretching and beginning to question your whereabouts and even who you are.

You are in this because you are part of God, and God is many things and infinite in behavior as well as wisdom. When you learn how this works you will no longer judge you for being on earth, or in matter. You are not really here anyway, so judgment is pretty much wasted energy. As you begin to learn how you got to this phase you will be thankful that you came. You are one of the newborn areas of creation and you are literally in the process of birth. Of course, everyone wants to get involved in a new process, so here we have you all... millions of you.

You hover about and rush about and even lie about. You are moving and mixing and shaking things up and becoming quite excited as time goes by. This is the part I want to discuss. This excitement is draining you and pulling you into other areas that are not high vibration. You actually feel more "alive" and like you are spinning and vibrating with life, but you are really spinning and vibrating with adrenaline. Adrenaline is pumped into you to keep you going. It is a stimulant and it is a drug.

So you see, you are actually drugging you by stimulation every time you create excitement for yourself.

New thrills, I believe you call it. This is how you keep your "zing" going. So; how can I get you to slow down and stop this zinging long enough to feel your pain and recognized that you have pain? This is the problem, because no one wants to uncover the mess that leads up to the pain. Everyone is dodging the subject and looking for a quick fix or easy cure.

I promise you now that if you will take the time to stop and "look," really "look," at who you are and what you carry, it will be the most rewarding and healing process you will ever undergo in this field of matter. There is nothing else. Go within and know who you are. Begin to look at you and how you are layered and you will be on the first step to recovering you for you. It is not as if you are not the one in charge of your life. You have free will. "You may stop and put your priorities in order or you may continue to play the creation game. That is to let everything be created by a higher intelligence and ignore the truth of matter, which is that you are the highest intelligence."

You are not here to continue with a game of hide and seek. You are here to wake up and rise up. Will you? Can you? Do you care?

❧

*W*e are now in a position to heal and if we take this opportunity we will be free of pain. This is the place where there is hope. This is the place where we have guided you. As you begin to assess the value of "letting go and letting God," you will be allowed to see the pain that you have carried and to know that you no longer *need* your pain to keep you safe.

You have been using your pain as a catalyst to prevent further pain. You use your pain to keep you safe. You hurt and you register this hurt as comforting and safe. Why? Because you have always hurt and are just numb to this fact. You have grown so accustomed to the pain that you would not know how you felt without it. It has always been there in the back of your mind to tell you to not do this or that, as it is dangerous and will stir up the pain that already exists in you. So you do not touch this or that, or partake of this or that, because your pain rules over you.

You go only on safe trips and you visit only safe places and safe people. You are led around by pain and it is an integral part of you. As you begin to see how your pain is simply a mechanism that is outdated, you will begin to allow joy its rightful place within you. You will find that joy may come, and you will no longer fear having joy. You will no longer fear that joy is not yours because you are pain and pain does not allow joy. You will know that it is safe to let go of your hold on pain and give joy a chance without running away in fear that this joy will create greater pain in the future.

You all do this. You all believe that the good will not last, so you must get it while you can; the love will not last, so you enjoy it while you can. It will last. From now on we are creating a world that is pain-free and filled with joy;

joy of life and joy of death, joy of poverty and joy of wealth, joy of starvation and joy of obesity. Joy is spontaneous and moves. In the same way that you can have pain of wealth or pain of starvation, you may have joy in the same areas. Joy travels to all dimensions and all levels of creation. If you are going to do it, do it with joy.

Now; when you lose your job, I want you to laugh. Look for the gift that you have just received. Maybe you will move to a much better place for you, or maybe you will have a very well-deserved vacation. So enjoy this time for you. Don't freak out about how you will create your next job and know that you are always creating what is best for you. So what if you end up out on the street with no home. Is this your fear? Well then, I suggest you go into it in order to release it. Are we here to grow in money and possessions, or are we here to grow in love? Love is allowing all to occur and knowing that it is best for the evolution of the soul.

So; what is best for the evolution of you? Is it best to sit in an office day after day from nine to five, or is it best to show yourself how you have survival skills? Then again, does it really matter? Do you have to do anything? No, you do not! It will all come to you. Everything that you are creating as a gift for you will be presented to you, so you need only to sit and wait for your good to be delivered. Please do not become frightened and lose sight of the gift. It is a present, it is not a bad thing and it is up to you to see it as you choose. Joy or pain!

≈⫯≈

*A*s we begin to rise above joy and pain, love and hate, bigotry and tolerance, we move into balance. One will no longer need to see the world as black or white, yellow or orange, purple or green. It will *be.* It will not be according to view, or description, or even tolerance levels. All will be tolerant as all will be *perceived* as God. God is tolerant. God is everything and everyone and every emotion or energy that you find in you or out of you. It is all God. Nothing exists outside of God. You are God and everyone else is God.

God is love and light, and God is what you view as darkness, vengefulness and hatred. Stop viewing it as hateful or dark and it will cease to be dark. You create the dark energy by calling it dark. Call it God. *Call everything God for this is the truth.*

You have waited so long to hear me speak to you and to know the truth. Do not turn away now. It is not often that I can move you into a position in which you are capable of seeing beyond good vs. evil, and your *strong* belief that good must triumph over all that is bad. Stop making anything bad and no one will *fight* anyone. Stop living in fear of being bad or wrong and you will surely come to the light of truth.

The truth is not an easy pill for you to swallow and even now you want me to speak to you of love and light and faith, so you will not feel the fear that I may be feeding you bad, or wrong, or evil information. You are too far down to see up. You are so full of fear and anxiety that you feel you must paint everything black or white, good or bad, love or hate. I started you in this series of books from your perspective and gave you what you needed in order to raise you to a new level of seeing creation. Love vs. evil was a very easy concept for you to grasp.

Well, we have graduated to the eleventh grade and now it is time to learn how nothing happens that is not part of God. Absolutely nothing can ever occur without God's permission. God is totally and infinitely responsible for every occurrence that could possibly exist or even not exist. *Do you judge God?*

꒰ᴥ꒱

*A*s you begin to move to a level of understanding that is more conducive to seeing from all perspectives, you will see how all is simply creation. No one is right, no one is wrong; no one is good, no one is bad. Everyone and everything is part of creation, no right or wrong exists. No one ever dies and you really have no sense of reality from where you stand.

You have only to look around you to know that you are in the middle of a maze and trying hard to find your way out. Your intuition will guide you out by showing you that you do not belong stuck in matter. You rise above matter in order to see clearly that this matter is not truth. Matter is the glue that is sticking you to situations and to one another. Let go of the material world and move up. You will find that in rising above a situation you can take yourself out of karma, or what you believe to be karma. In rising up you can take yourself out of the melodrama and the fight or struggle to survive. Rise above and you see from above.

Now; as you begin to see how you create all that you are currently living in, you will understand that in the same way that you created it you can uncreate it, or see it from a new perspective. This is how I wish you to stay calm. Simply change your mind about how you see you. See yourself as a very adept caretaker and your one job is to care for you, not your lover, not your child, not your parent, but you. You are now in charge of loving and caring for you.

You will find that as you begin to know you better, you will learn your little tricks that you have devised over the years to protect your true identity and keep you safe. You see, most of you really believe that you are bad and did something wrong in the distant past. If you are defensive in conversations you are most likely defending yourself, so you won't be discovered as the bad person that you really believe yourself to be. As you go along you will discover that you hide your (what you believe to be) faults behind your moral beliefs. If you believe you are bad in some way you may take on a very rigid sense of moral issues. This entitles you to be seen by others as a good and righteous individual. Therefore you will never be suspected as being the villain that you believe you are hiding from them.

This is the game you all play. Do you consciously play it? Sometimes, but mostly you are hiding and do not know that you are. As you travel through your own inner self you begin to learn how you judge you and how you see you. Look to your mirrors and you will get a good idea of how you see yourself. If you see others as bad or awful, guess what? You are seeing and judging you as bad or awful. You cannot see what is not in you. If you do not trust them, you do not trust you.

How do you develop a greater sense of your own hidden aspects? Look! Look into you and ask yourself questions. You may even write down your answers since, in this class, we all know how to communicate with our soul. So you may find your answers and rise above cause and effect by rising above *belief*. Let go of belief. Do not believe in anything, as it is impossible to have only one perspective or purported truth, when in reality all is truth. So how can you possibly see things from tunnel vision? Look out and up not down and into matter.

As you learn to rise above matter, you will learn how it is your clay to mold. This is the part you will really enjoy. This is where you learn that you are not the victim or the matter. You are the one who creates. You are God and this is *your life as God!*

*W*hen we first began to teach love we did not know how much you knew regarding this ability. It is not only 'not' an ability it is not an emotion. Love is what is and love is what will always be. Love is not measured by what you call one's ability to love or not to love. Love comes as it is, with no strings attached. Love does not come with requirements. You are love and love is how you are. You are no longer in a position to not want love.

As you learn that you are love, you learn that you are also afraid of love. You were taught that love was something else, so when someone says, "I love you," you remember your first lesson with "I love you." Did you get hit or spanked by someone who said "I am doing this because I love you?" If so, you now have hitting in your definition of love. Were you sexually abused or were you screamed at by the one who taught you to love? Do you now have abusive behavior attached to your definition of what love is? Do you now repeat what you were taught, by doing it out of love when it is actually not very loving at all?

This is the teaching that must end. Nothing is done out of love of another. Everything that you do you do out of "fear of" or "belief in." You spank or hit a child for running in the street because you are *afraid* the child will be injured. You do not hit a child because you love them. Please begin to tell the truth to the new generation. You are hitting or striking them out of fear. How do you expect children to grow up and know the difference between love and fear? "I love you so I hit you" is a lie. "I love you because you are love," is the truth. "I hit you out of fear of you being in danger," is the truth. Now when your child grows up he or she will not be looking for a love partner who loves him or her by hitting him or her, be it verbally or physically.

So; if you have been hitting and making it out to be love, you are now informed. Look into your past. Where did you learn your definition of love and is it true or is it a lie? How often have you searched for love and ended up with abusive behavior? You are looking for what you were taught. If you were sexually abused by the one who professed to love you, you may find that you run like hell the minute someone says, "I love you." This is a child who knows that love means danger. Danger was attached to the "I love you's."

So, where do you stand on love? How do you know what to ask for, when what you are asking for is what you believe to be different than what you were taught? You all ask for love, yet you do not consider what your definition of love is. Why not stop asking for love and begin to accept that you really are love? You will find that when you ask for love, you are asking for a return to the nest where you first learned what love is. Ask to know you and ask to see how you are love.

You are not so much out of step with love as you are out of step with yourself. When you really get to know you, you will really begin to appreciate being you. You will see you as a true being of light with no wrong or bad. Everything just is... even love!

As we began to teach you about love, we realized that, to you, love was simply a desire, a feeling, or an emotion. It is important to realize that love is what you are and that love is also what you search for. You are searching for you. I am well aware that you do not understand the concepts that are given in this series of books. It is not that you cannot yet perceive such concepts, it is more that you are not able to see through your own love.

Most of you will find that as you grow in awareness your love grows. You are your love and as you grow so grows love. Love will cover your entire existence as soon as you tune in and see only through the eyes of love. Love is very much like compassion. It is not so much a way of feeling as it is an ability to accept and know. Knowledge can be a very powerful and uplifting experience. All knowledge has power and all power is yours.

As you begin to rise to a new perspective, you will find it unacceptable to no longer accept you as love. You will find that you do not allow you to be love as you are busy being discomfort, and pain, and judgment, and ridicule. You are so afraid to be who you really are, as you are afraid of being left behind for your worthlessness. Most of what you consider to be worthy is not. You are worshiping false idols and making everyone and everything

more important than you. And who are you? Of course...
you forgot didn't you?

So, as you move along in your day to day
experience, I wish you to learn how to be love and see love.
Can you spend an entire day focusing only on love? Can
you spend one day looking for love in everyone and
everything? Can you find love today? Is love in you or do
you find yourself left out where love is concerned? How do
you recognize love? You will know it when you see it, as it
will be a reflection of you.

⚜

*W*hen you begin to understand how you are God,
you will begin to know how you do not sin. You will know
that you are above reproach and that you do no wrong.
Until then you will continue to abuse you and punish you
in order to control you. You have taught yourself how to
control you by means of self-punishment, and various parts
of you are well aware of the price to pay for every crime or
sin.

You are so accustomed to your own handed down
punishment that you no longer *feel* like you are being
punished. "Oh, this feels like my life has always felt. It's
just like me to never win." This is the vibration you live
under. You do not rise above this vibration as you may not
know how to. You are so afraid of being displeased or

disappointed that you do not give you too much good. After all, you don't really believe that you deserve that much good, because your programming tells you how bad you are.

When you begin to clear this portion of you, you may feel a bit depressed and even unhappy. You will be peeling away all the layers of you that you most dislike about you. So it can get a bit unsettling for you, and you may even wish to end it all just to put you out of your misery. At times you won't even know why you are so miserable, but it will pass as you peel off this layer of mistrust of self that has kept you in control of your other selves for such a long time.

With insight comes clarity and with clarity you can see. I tell you what to expect in order to help you ease through this period of adjusting to being less of you, or peeling away your unnecessary garbage. When you get to this point of not caring if you live or die and not wanting to put up with being in your life any longer, you have crossed over from self-love to self-loathing, and from here you will move back into balance. Self-loathing is simply a part of you that is no longer necessary. It is not necessary to carry your self-hatred into our bright new future.

So, be patient with yourself should you come face to face with this part of you. You are only clearing an old belief that taught you, you were less than perfect. You are not "less" than perfect and you are not awful. If you feel like your life is awful it is a pretty clear indication that you believe that you are awful. It is in you and being reflected outward. What else do you see outside of you, because this too is inside reflecting back at you?

I hope you know that you are loved. You are not ugly and you are not loathsome. You are true love and real beauty and you are God being born in matter. Sometimes in this birthing process there are a few rough spots and lots of crying. It will all be okay soon. You have come so far and you are simply healing the core of you; the stuff that has taken root and is affecting all that is. It is best to get rid of your garbage now, as you will not need it in your future. It has no purpose other than to hold you down and control you. It is not what we need to rise up. It will not last as it is not the truth and, in this class, we are taking-on only the truth.

♦

*F*or as long as time has been, you have been. You are not the only one who is here in that you are part of a whole. There is a big picture and you are part of it. Most of what you believe to be you is actually part of the illusion.

For example, you believe yourself to be afraid of being harmed, however, it is impossible to be harmed. You believe yourself to be afraid of being alone yet it is impossible to be alone. It is virtually not a possibility. You believe yourself afraid of being "out in the streets" and that too is illusion. You may end up living in the streets, but you will not be any less than you are now. How is this – you shout! You are you and whether you have money, or clothes, or a roof over your head, you will still be you. You will not stop being unsafe by holding on to a lot of money, or a car, or a home. You will only stop feeling unsafe by letting go of your fear concerning protection. You are afraid of being unprotected and this leads to all anxiety concerning your welfare.

When you begin to feel safe you will no longer need protection and you will be free to walk the streets without fear. You will know that God is in you and you are in God. As you go along you will learn how God does not wish you to be so afraid. Lay down your fears and trust that God is taking care of your basic spiritual needs. God is tugging at the garbage bag that you carry and saying, "No, you don't really need this defense mechanism. You may let go of this for now and see how it feels to be free of it."

As you begin to lay down all the unnecessary defense mechanisms and protective devices that you have used for so long to keep you safe, you will find that you not only feel freer, you feel better about your security. Your security becomes a matter for your own God-self and no longer a matter for police and guns and laws of protection. I want you to lay down your fire arms and your defense mechanisms, that you have built around you to protect you from harm. You have an entire suit of armor and not only does it keep everyone out and away from you; it keeps you out and away from you.

You must learn to walk through life unprotected and know that you are as safe without protection as you are with it. You are actually safer without it, as I am allowed into you when you let down your protective walls and allow all to enter. You may spend your life in fear or you may say, "Okay God, I let go, I'm yours!" You are not the first to be afraid to let go and not worry about what tomorrow will bring, but do not fear, I am not going to leave you as it is impossible for God to leave you. You may shut me out, but I will be waiting the minute the door is reopened.

As I wait to re-enter, I will be guiding from behind or outside of this wall you have built to keep you safe and keep everyone else at bay. You will find that as your walls come tumbling down you will be much safer than you have ever been before. You will be standing alone and stripped and shining like a star about to streak across the heavens. This last layer is the one that matters most. If you can let go without harming yourself, you have come home. You are outside the gate to heaven, but the gates and walls are yours not God's. God never locked anyone out of heaven. Man created his own defenses to shut himself down and out. Now is the time to unlock the doors and let go of protection. You do not need protection as there is no danger. Danger is part of the end of illusion and the illusion must fall in order for the truth to stand.

So; don't be afraid. Walk out into the world without this one bag of garbage and trust in your own God-self. You are not afraid of God are you? You trust God don't you? Come on now, let go and I will hold you up!

❧

So far you have not been capable enough to care for yourself. You feel inadequate in this area and so you search in vain for others to fulfill this chore for you. You do not wish to be responsible for your own self and so you constantly shift responsibility for yourself onto others. Then you get all upset when others do not wish to be responsible for your feelings and emotions. You are giving you away and you do not know that you are. You are no longer capable of being in charge of your own garbage so you push responsibility for it onto others. You say, "Oh, this is painful and he or she is causing my pain, so I must change he or she." You cannot change him or her. It is impossible to change another. Yes, you may yell and scream until you get *your* way and he or she may begin to listen, but that is their choice and they are changing and you have no responsibility and no credit to gain.

If you are not sure about who you are and who you are not, I suggest you begin to look into your mirror and you will see very quickly whether or not you are holding your own or pushing it off on others. You will find that you most often do not like the ones who reflect what you do not like most in you. You will find that as you begin to watch your reflections you will no longer feel the need to accuse, or demand, or change another. You will learn to accept all as part of you, as all are reflecting some part of you.

Now; when you begin to know that you are no longer the creation, but that you are the creator, you will more than likely begin to take better care of you. You will begin to know that you are the one who reflects out and you are the one who then turns around and judges what you have recently reflected. You will find also that you no longer know how you separate you from your reflection, as you have become attuned to the fact that all comes from you and not at you.

This is the key to success in your world. Remember that it begins and ends with you. It starts and finishes with you. You send it out and it manifests in matter and returns to you in form. Then you get upset because you do not like how this person is behaving. He or she is doing this or that and it is simply *you* doing this or that *within*.

When you begin to heal, you will begin to take off layers of old dysfunctional behavior. You will begin to reek with your own rotten behavioral system. You will stir up garbage that has been untouched for many years and sometimes many lifetimes. Do not freak out as you begin to draw to you what you are. You are simply cleaning out the closets of you and you may find some pretty strange stuff in there. And since it is *in* you, it will reflect out and manifest and you will think, "Oh my God, I've really lost it now." You *have* lost it and are losing it. You are losing pounds and pounds of unnecessary waste and you are moving to a better level of seeing creation.

So; as you begin to see how dysfunctional you really are please do not get too upset. Do not be afraid that you are going down instead of up. Down is where you have been without knowing it and up is where you are now moving. The strange thing is that this will feel the opposite for you. You will feel like you are falling apart and losing it when, in actuality, you are gaining by letting go of, or lifting up by dropping off your dead weight.

Either way you are in a win/win situation. You are winning you back from the dark. You are winning love as you have never known love and you are winning the knowledge and the wisdom of God. You cannot lose in this time of change. With each loss, that you believe you see, you are actually rising. You go up each time you take off. How can losing be bad? What are you so upset about? Don't you want to lose? It's the best thing you can do. Lose it all. Let it all go. Become nothing!

*A*s you begin to realize your own greatness you will begin to know how you fit into the big picture. The more you become God the less you become an individualized identity. You are learning to merge your ego identity within the God force. You are losing you and you are becoming God.

Now; as this emergence becomes stronger, you may be stretched in order to survive this transition. It may be necessary to make you fit, so to speak, into God. You are now form; and form is determined to stand its ground and not be controlled or taken over. It is best to *allow* this takeover. You will not feel it as love at the instant you begin to stretch, as part of you will be so busy resisting that you will not be able to focus on the part that is nonresistant and love. Hold on to the idea of love and you will find that you have less resistance. The more you fight this takeover the more exhausted you become, and soon you will give up and give in and allow God to take over.

The reason the takeover will not feel good and godlike is simply because *you* do not at this moment believe yourself to be good and godlike. So, as you are drawn *forward*, you will actually feel as though you have fallen through a long dark hole that is very frightening for you. You are not falling and losing control of the light. You are rising and shaking and quaking with the *shift* that is occurring within you. You are shifting gears and this new speed of vibration is a little difficult for you to adjust to. You will feel as though you have taken a nose-dive and you will wish to know that you are simply approaching lift-off. You are not falling, you are rising. You are not awful, you are wonderful. Life is not awful to you; you are just seeing the awfulness that you think you are.

We are clearing out what is not necessary and moving you into position for take off. You will begin to ascend by moving forward into spirit, not by moving backward into matter. As you leave, the weightiness of matter will *hold* you to the ground while the liftoff of spirit will raise you up. You are now in quite a predicament aren't you? You can't go forward and you can't go back. You are in transition and you will never be the same again. Mostly I want you to remember that you must hold your head up high no matter what. You are God and God is landing on planet Earth in you. Not in Arizona, not in London, not in Japan, not in Russia. God is landing in the each and every one of you. You will never see another landing quite like this one. It is remarkable how well you have *received* this entire message. You are truly exceptional in your ability to adapt to the light of God.

I did not begin to write these books with all knowledge of their outcome. This is an experiment in communication from God to his children. "Can they hear me?" I mused. "Will they accept me and will they understand any portion of the truth?" I see now that God has the ability to speak freely to those who will listen and God has the ability to transform energy into words on a page. It is wonderful to see you grow and change and it is my gift to you as I become one with you.

You are the one I have come to know as me. I am communicating with me through one of my own without much difficulty. This is good, this is God and God is you. You have carried yourself well and you are in a very prime point in time. You must not be afraid to move forward. I know how much you want to run back toward safety of matter and form, but you will so enjoy spirit and light. You can float, you can fly, you can soar once you have let go of the deadly weights you carry. Come on now, put down that belief in punishment, and revenge, and good guys, and bad guys. You don't require such nonsense any longer.

You are very profoundly affected by this game of light and dark, good and bad. We will walk forward and know that we do not live in duality, we live in harmony. We do not live in stress and fear; we live in peace and love. It is just ahead my sweet child. Take the plunge. Move into your future with nothing to hold on to but God and your trust.

✺

Now that you are learning how it feels to change, you are not so certain you like it. It is not a punishment; it is a letting go of your belief in punishment. It is a letting go of your believe in pain, and a letting go of your belief that you are bad. As you let go of these beliefs you will see what you are letting go of. If you carry heavy judgment you will be heavy – if you do not you will not be heavy. You have accumulated enough fear and judgment to hold you down for eons. You are now moving what is solidified from the past and it is very hard to move. Do not be upset when it takes a little time to get it up and off you. It is stuck to you like hard cement and the melting away will take a while.

Be patient when you clear. Know that you are moving to a new perspective which is an all seeing perspective or point of view. You are broadening your perspective to carry all sides of any situation into view. You will be able to see not only both sides of a single situation, but everything in between. This may amaze and exhaust you at first, for you will be emotionally attached to each point of view as you settle into it. But you will not stick to it nor will you rush ahead to the next point, until you have cleared the emotions attached to the point you are now clearing.

This is a process by which you get to see all sides of everything, and your confusion will come at not being able to settle on one definite way of handling the situation. One day you will be determined to do it this certain way and the next day you may change your mind completely and go with the opposite view. Then again, by day three you may find another way to handle your current dilemma. This will continue until you no longer feel the need to be set in one way or another way. You will see *all* ways and decide to wait and see what will happen.

You will stop creating from determination and from goal oriented fashion, and begin to turn your creating over to God. You will begin to trust that God wants to give you his gifts, and should you decide to receive them you will sit and wait patiently for his gifts to be delivered. One of your biggest problems on earth is instant gratification. You want what you want and not what God wants, and you want it right now. This is addiction. This is baby needs, baby wants, and if baby doesn't get it right now, baby will scream and cry and make a big fuss so everyone will give baby what baby wants.

Why does baby want what baby wants? You are on the material plane and the draw to this plane is material satisfaction and material greed. It is not a known or acknowledged-by-any greed, but it is here. It is a need to constantly fulfill the urges of the physical body, which is set in motion through the nervous system, by an overloaded emotional body that has been unloading on the physical for eons. The emotional body is attached to your physical body and it cries out in pain from its own need to be healed. It yells, "Heal me, fix me." So you come in kicking and screaming and looking for a quick fix.

Could it be a Band-Aid you are looking for? Could it be something greater than a bit of candy to make baby feel better in the moment. Could it be maybe something more than a spending spree at your favorite store, or that new car that fixed your hurt emotions for just about six months? Could it be more than an expensive night out on the town that would make it all feel better for as long as a week, or could it be winning that big lottery that would fix the hurt for a bigger length of time? You all want your quick fixes, and whether it's pain in the physical body or pain in the emotional body it is still an illusion, which makes the quick fix also an illusion.

You are looking for you; you are not looking for a Band-Aid. You will find you by looking into you and digging you out from all that garbage that is suffocating you. You will not find you in money or in matter. You are right here inside of you. You will not find your help from the outside. It is impossible to find you outside of you. You are looking for love, not a lottery win, not a chocolate bar, not a drug or a drink. It is you, you are so hurt over. You are not hurt over what anyone has ever done to you. You are hurt over what you have done to you. Can't you see that? Don't you know why the baby screams in pain? The baby wants freedom from the burden of the emotional and physical manifested pain. The pain came from constant abuse and pushing *down* of the self by the self.

You are so accustomed to going down into *more* pain and *more* drugs to heal the pain, or shut it up, that you think it is awful to be you. It is not awful to be you and if you feel awful it is from the withdrawal process. When you lose your habits you go into withdrawal and you get the shakes and your body will kick and scream. Many of you are in treatment for your old addictions to many, many things, and your body is kicking and screaming because it wants its habits and drugs and old programming back. This too shall pass. All will heal and you will stand new and refreshed when you have crossed the last barrier into you.

You may find yourself on shaky legs until you adjust to this new you, but the new you will not be addicted. The new you will be free from attachments of any kind. The new you will begin to see you, the you who was buried under all that garbage, the you who is the light of your beingness. And what do you see in others when you are seeing the light in you? Right! You will see light in everyone, everything and every situation.

Won't that feel good? Aren't you tired of seeing the bad in your life, don't you want to see the other side for a change? It won't take as long as you believe. It is why you came here. You came here to transform and to move through dimensions at will. Well, you are now moving and the more you take off, the less weight you carry, the higher you will fly.

*I*t is time to become you and keep all of you for you. It is not wrong to be love and light and it is not wrong to keep *your* love and light. It is you who is in this for you and you are in this to heal you. You will find that you not only do not see yourself through the eyes of love, you do not give to yourself. I want you to begin to give to you. You are the most important person in your life and you cannot ignore you any longer.

Once you begin to give to you, you will see how you will grow from your own nurturing. You will begin to blossom and rise above all that is not nurturing and loving. You will begin to know that to love yourself is the biggest thing you can or will do. It is not a difficult task, as you are lovable, but you will make it a very big job, as you believe you are so unlovable. This is how I want you to handle this big job. For the first few months I want you to simply get up in the morning and look at yourself in the mirror and say, "I love you." You will not have such a hard time with this as you have already learned to do this in the past.

Next, I want you to become aware of the fact that God loves you and God believes in you enough to shed light on you. You will find that this part is no more difficult than the part about saying "I love you." So, after you have said "I love you," I want you to hug yourself and thank God for shedding light on you. Then you may begin your day and remember throughout your day that you are loved by God and God is all that matters. Nothing else matters during this time. It is God and you. We are one you and I. You do not need anyone or anything. You have all that you already need. God is you and you are God.

When you get to the point that the stretching begins, simply hug God close to you and hold on for dear life, because God is your life. God is all that you are and all that you will ever need. You are total and complete as you are and you only *think* that you are less than. You are no more or less than God. You are all that is God. You will find that as you move through you, you will see all sides of you and you will freak out at what you are, because what you are is a combination of all that has ever touched you. Do not freak out. Let it be. Let everything be you and everyone else be who they are which, of course, is also a combination of everything that they have ever touched.

You are all dysfunctional in some way. This simply means that you are not functioning at full capacity and some of you are barely functioning at all. You are lights and you are not shining, you are simply sitting in a very dark place. I will turn you on. I will light your fire. I will guide you through the darkness and debris that is hiding you from life. You are not meant to be in darkness or confusion. It is okay to know the truth and the truth has power over the lie. It is okay to see what is going on around you. You have been hiding in a corner of darkness for so long that now you hurt when you see light. You will adjust. This is not the bad stuff, this is the good stuff.

It is okay to know the truth and it is okay to pull away from the lie you have always lived under. You are no longer going to depend on others for your truth. You are going to follow you, as you will know that you intuitively carry your own guidance system. It is okay to pull away from the beliefs you have owned for so long. It is okay to see everything differently. It is okay to be afraid to stand stripped of your old patterns and protective belief system. You will be much better for having left this weight behind you.

You are no longer being seen as you once were, because you are no longer seeing creation as you once did. When you break away it shows in your eyes. It is now beginning to show and you will affect those who do not wish to wake up just by the light you shine. Some will want to remove themselves from your presence as you will frighten them. They wish to sleep and they do not want the light on while they sleep. If you are shunned it is always best to let it go. If you are accepted it is because you are like vibration.

Do not worry so much about how you will fit in and be accepted. Once you have learned to love you, you will not care who does or does not accept you. Once you have learned to love you, you will move to a new level of *seeing* everything else. You will no longer *need* them, for you will already have someone. This someone you will have is you. You will feel so good about having you that you will be amazed!

*S*o far you are not afraid to be you so much as you are afraid you will not be accepted as you. You are so sure that if you become who you really are no one will accept you. You are afraid that you will lose friends and be alone. It is not wrong to be you and you are not bad. The whole purpose of being who you really are is so that you will find those who are also like you. How can you move to your right place if you hold on to an identity that is not yours and sit in a position that is no longer valid?

Some of you have stayed, with those you were once drawn to, out of loyalty or fear of letting go. It is okay to let go and move ahead and leave those behind who are not yet moving. It is okay to allow everyone to be who they are, without blaming them for not being who you think they should be. It is okay to allow everyone to be and to allow you to be. This is one of the toughest ones for you to get. Once you let you be who you are, you automatically let everyone else be who they are.

As you move along inside of you, you will find that you are *constantly* changing and fluctuating. You are breathing in and out to a rhythm and it is pulsating in you. You fluctuate, so how can you possibly stay in one identity or fixed idea of how you should be? Move, change, shift, experience all sides, every phase of life is different and it is up to you to experience what you are. You vibrate and you fluctuate to the extent that you are no longer who you were last year. You have changed. You are a different person than you were two years ago. How do you expect to stay attached to specific likes or dislikes or people or places? You are constantly moving and shifting. Flow with that, do not fight it.

Now; when you begin to get *stuck*, or set in your ways, you are stopping the fluctuation that you are. You are stopping the intake and outflow. You are cutting off what keeps you going and it eventually kills you. You get stuck in "your way" and can't move, and you dig in deeper, and eventually you die. It is like getting a car stuck in the mud and the wheels spin and mud flies and you refuse to try a new technique. You just sit there in the driver's seat, with your foot on the gas, trying as hard as you can to make your car run. You are stuck in mud. You ran into a hole and you're getting in deeper.

Take your foot off the gas. Stop pressing down on you. You are pushing you into the mud and spinning your tires to no avail. Give it up and get out and walk. Try a new way. Stop pretending that you can only go in one direction. You have many choices, and if you are stuck it is because you refuse to see that you are in charge. By accepting that you are in charge you will learn that you can take whichever course feels best for you. Do not sit in your car and wait for a tow truck, because you did not create a phone to call on yet. It's all up to you. You may give up on all the options and sit and spin your wheels until you expire into death, or you may choose your path or your way back home.

No one is asking you to get out of the car and dig it out of the mud with your bare hands. That is, of course, an option, but it is not the only option. You create your choices and you negate your choices. You could fill a phone book with all the choices available to you in a single day. Your problem is you are stuck and afraid to make a choice because you may make the wrong choice, so you have simply stopped living and started dying. You all do this. There is no one who is not dying on earth. You have choices. A child begins to die as he enters the earth because he is told to die. Stop telling lies. You do not need to die nor do you need to live.

It's all a big dream. There are no people. There are ideas and energy and change and transformation and light and more energy; energy enough to do whatever you want in the way of creation. What shall you create today? What is your choice? You name it. You are coming to the crossroads of your existence and learning that you need not do anything or you may do everything. It is simply a matter of choice. Create for you, not for someone else. Who do you want to be? Who do you think you are? How can you mold a lump of clay and know ahead of time exactly how your creation will look? You mold and create as you go because your ideas change as you fluctuate, so you change as you fluctuate.

It is okay to change and is okay to not change. It is okay to be who you are now and it is okay to change to something else. It is God in his most glorious design. God is a creation of his own creating and it is good and wonderful to behold. You are this great God who creates through you each day and each year as you pulsate and fluctuate. You are magnificent in your splendor. You can create it anyway you want it. Do not be afraid to want what is already yours.

You are in a time of great duality and this duality is about to give way to freedom. No more pushing and pulling, hitting and kicking, slapping and groaning. The worst is over and you will be welcoming you with open arms. You will be so happy to discover you, that you will rejoice for days when you finally see your true splendor. It has not been said before, but I will say it now. God does not exist. How can I say this to you? You must remember that *all* possibilities are acceptable and real and illusion. So what is this thing called God?

❧

*A*s far as I can see you are love. You have never 'not' been love. So; how do you get this idea that you are not what I see that you are? Maybe you simply do not understand what love is. Love is not a decision to accept someone as a mate and love is not a choice about what feels good and what does not. Love is a powerful and unexplained lightness about you. Not about someone else, but about you. Love is you. Love is accepting you and allowing you to be who you are.

The reason that you choose to fall in love with certain individuals is because they see what they want in you. You like that they "want" you because it says, "I accept you," and so you marry or live with them. They may not be the source of your light feeling, but you are going to hold on to them for dear life because they make you feel good. The only thing is that you are the one who makes you glow and feel good. You do it by accepting their statement of affection and acceptance. If you were to discover that they not only treated you with this loving attitude and acceptance, but that they lavishly accepted and loved all who crossed their path you would no longer feel so loved by them.

Why is this? Why is it that you cannot share this feeling with others? Why is it that you must harness and own the one who complements you and shares moments of privacy with you? Why can you only own one another and not share? It is because you are so afraid of losing. You are afraid of not having love, or those light feelings that you lock in with the one who makes you feel good and you want to keep them all to yourself. This is how mating began. It was an agreement between two individuals who shared good feelings and they decided to not do it with anyone else. They decided to keep it to themselves, so obviously they had something very good going.

These types of choices are just that. No one asks you to be locked into wedlock without you choosing it for your own reasons. Usually there is a great deal of fear surrounding these types of relationships; either afraid of having or afraid of not having. It is up to you how you wish to live your life, it is not up to another so do not judge or blame another for your choices. Know that you always have the choice of changing your mind and no one is a prisoner without asking to be. If you are in a situation you no longer feel good in, leave. Why stay if it does not feel good to you. Do not be afraid to move on and to change.

You are moving into a situation in time and space where everyone and everything is to change. This is movement and flexibility. This is moving and flowing and it is knowing that you are not trapped, you are only stuck in the mud and spinning your wheels. It is not such a long path to walk as you believe. You will know who you are and how you wish to be you, and you will know that God is shining his light on you. So why worry about getting your light ignited by someone else. God is taking care of you and you are loved by God.

❧

I am now going to discuss how you treat your own self. You treat you very, very poorly and I wish you to stop. You have come to a place that is not good for lying and you must begin to tell you the truth now. The truth is not that painful and it's time to accept it and to come out of denial. The truth is basically that you do not like you, so you have contemptible thoughts regarding you. Anytime you have a bad thought regarding someone who you believe to be bad, or awful, or mean; it is you having a thought or belief that says, "I am bad, or awful, or mean and I must hide it."

It is not that you are bad or awful or mean. You have all the energy in you from past lives and you *know*, on some level, that you killed or beheaded or brutalized. So, as a soul, you came in this life promising not to brutalize or kill or punish in an offensive fashion. And each time you *feel* your own inadequacy to control your natural urge to kill or punish, you rise up inside yourself to try to control these urges. This causes great stress on the nervous system and then you get all upset or angry, and usually at someone else.

You are controlling your urges and tendencies to destructive behavior through the use of submissive behavior and it is killing you. You are learning to be polite and accept criticism because you want to learn, as a species, how to rise up above the tendency to kill. You are then upset with you for not allowing you permission to strike out; and you are upset with the other person for making you want to strike out. You are so upset with yourself for wanting to strike out, or get revenge, that you then get upset with the other person so he or she will not see your murderous intent. It is in all of you. You are part of nature. Fight for survival is strong in you. You are beating yourself up emotionally for being what you are.

I want you to learn to trust your instincts. Do not rush out and kill because you feel the urge to kill. Do, however, trust your intuition when it says, "This is not a good place to be." It will always behoove you to trust you. This is the only way to be you and the entire goal here is to *accept* who you are. You are God and you are experimenting in matter. Be you, be God and experiment away. It is not wrong and it is not always fun. You have lost your sense of humor in all of this creating business and now it's time to relax a little and stop judging you for your life and instincts and loving.

Yes. You even judge you for loving. "Oh no, is he the wrong one or is she the wrong one?" Does it matter? Love whoever you want for as long to you want. It is only a way of shining your light on another and your light is your light. Your light *is* you, and you *are* your light. So put your light on anyone it pleases you to touch. If it feels good do it! If it doesn't, don't! Very simple logic and yet so difficult to accept.

So; as you go about your day today, I want you to remember that you own you. You control you. You live and die in you and you may make all choices concerning you. You may put you anywhere you want. You have charge of you and you have control over you. You have learned in this class how other parts of you are controlling you and you have learned how you are controlling and pushing them back. I highly suggest that you begin to work together toward a common goal.

Why not start accepting *all* parts of you and begin to get along with you. You are pulling and pushing at all your traits and characteristics and you are killing you in the struggle. Stop trying to make part of you acceptable and part of you not. You are all acceptable and so is your programming. You are part of everything that taught you and trained you and touched you and so what! Let it be. Let you be who you are. Stop trying to put part of you *down*. The idea here is to bring you *up*. You want to rise don't you? You want to ascend to a new level of total awareness don't you? If you do, you will accept all parts of you and you will stop pushing back those parts you call awful. They too will rise with you.

There is no awful or bad or wrong in this class. It is all a perspective and if you choose to continue to see it as bad you will get to. You see... you always get what you ask for. Choice! It is all a matter of choice.

❧

As far as I can tell from here, it is rather difficult for you to become what you already are. You seem to have great difficulty becoming light. It is not so much that you fight it; it is more that you push it away. Darkness is so thick in you that it literally pushes back the light.

So; let's discuss darkness. Darkness is of one or two origins. Mostly it is fear and secondly it is reflected fear. It is not so much that you fear light as it is that you fear being what you do not know or understand. You have a preconceived idea of what the light should be and how it should feel. It is necessary at this time to let go of all preconceived ideas and begin to live in the moment. Do not project into a future situation to see how it may or may not suit you. Stay in this moment and watch for your life to unfold.

It is not so important that you become light as it is that you begin to *realize* that you already are light. As you begin to walk into the light you will begin to have faith that God is protecting you and caring for you and guiding you. As you do this you will learn that you are actually taking care of you with no guidance from anyone but you. As you learn to guide you in this fashion you will begin to trust you once again. It is not so much that you don't know how to trust you; it's more that you have never trusted you since you came into matter. This has to do with the fact that you came into a place with emotion, and emotion is not always pleasant for you.

So; you are not so sure that you have given you a gift by putting you in your current situation. This is why I always tell you to look for the gift. You are giving yourself the gift of bearing the light that will transform this planet. It is a great and awesome gift. You are totally free to choose giving birth or not giving birth. It is your choice and it has little-to-nothing to do with anything that is currently operating in this system. It is a choice of being or not being a light carrier. It is not so much a choice of bringing in God or God will be left out, because God is God with or without you.

If you choose to be a light bearer and to carry the seed to full term, you will do so. If you choose to not participate and to sit back and watch then that is the role you will play. Not everyone takes part in exactly the same fashion. Some watch, some assist and some are not interested. This is how all creation works. You get involved through choice and if it is not your choice you do not participate. Choices may be changed and scripts rewritten at any time. This is why I tell you to be flexible and to flow.

This is why I guide you to one side of the thought and back to the other.

As you began to read this series of books you were taught that my cows wanted off the planet simply because you are killing and eating all the animals. This is true and is only one way of looking at it or only one perspective. Since that time I have discussed living and dying, and given you permission to live or to die without any claim of wrong-doing. You may kill another and know that no one ever dies. Isn't that taking you to both sides of the same truth? Do you see now how even the lie is the truth. Everything you see and believe becomes your truth, so I try to show you more than simply your current painful way of seeing all your choices.

In our first three books I gave you a twin soul because you *need* so desperately to hang on to someone and be part of someone and even own someone. Now I have told you that you need no one and you never owned anyone and you are the only one here and it is all an illusion. You are in a dream and you are *thinking* all of this into existence. So; if this is a dream, what is the point in having anyone or anything of your own?

You see, I do not want you hanging on, so I convince you to let go. This gives you freedom of choice. You get to see all sides of every part of the entire spectrum. I choose to give you what you can handle and now I think you can handle more. You are not God and God does not exist. You are nothing and you are no one. Now how did that *feel?* Do you feel lost at those words? You see, nothing has occurred in your life this moment and yet your mood has fluctuated because of what you believe and what you have just been told. Your emotional body is going crazy trying to put this into perspective and carry forward this information to the rest of you.

You are told that you are someone and I have told you repeatedly that you are God and God is good. As I tell you the opposite you feel lost and without identity. I want you to realize how the emotion of fear-of-loss can change your entire view of both yourself and others. You project your image out *onto* others and then when they displease you, you take back what you have projected out and you try to find a new subject to project your pleasing attitude onto. This is why in the beginning of any relationship it feels very good. You are both projecting pleasant thoughts and hooking a "good guy" sign on one another.

Then, after the relationship has grown into wisdom of one another, you begin to take back all the pleasant images you projected out to that individual because you are not getting what you want from them, or because you *discovered* that this individual has an identity of his own or her own and your projected identity is simply that, *"your"* projection. So, now that you no longer wish to accept and make this individual yours, you begin to pull back and take back the identity you had painted on them. Now they feel hurt and rejected and unwanted and lost. Just as you did when I said, "You are not God; you are no one and nothing."

You are not so much feeling what is, you are feeling words. You are making information into feelings and attaching an identity to the information. You are not your identity; you are not your words. You are. You simply are.

⚜

You are not so much afraid of living as you are afraid of the truth. You judge certain situations as awful and you do not wish to accept what you believe to be awful. So you push anything that you judge as awful into a place of denial so you will not have to accept it as part of you. You are now at a point in creation where if you have been denying the truth it will be magnified for you. You must begin to see all aspects of you and those you choose to project an identity onto.

So; who are those you project this identity or image out to? Look toward those you are most attached to. When you begin to see their true colors you get upset because you were painting them a different color. You are not using your intuitive skills to see who they really are. You simply said, "Oh, this is how this person is and I like it so I will keep him or her." Next, after years maybe, you discover that this person is not this color and you begin to refocus on him or her to see how they are truly colored.

Once you have seen how they are truly colored, you usually reject or accept this new identity that you think you have just discovered. In actuality, you are changing color every second with your vibration. And eventually you will be seen as new. So, as you go along and discover how you have misconstrued how someone actually is (out of your own inability to accept certain identities into your perspective) I wish you to remember that this is simply a game you are playing with yourself. It is called denial and it is big.

As you begin to uncover your own denial you will begin to see what it is about yourself that you cannot accept. You will know, by looking closely at those you reject and those you accept, how you reject and accept certain aspects of your own beingness. The idea here is to learn to accept and allow all parts to be, because all parts are God.

⚜

*A*s long as you are learning to be your own God-self, you may as well remember that each of you is God. You are all God. No one is less than God. I know you don't agree from where you stand (or your perspective) but this is the truth of the matter. No one is less than God and all are becoming God. It is not so much a matter of seeing life as God; it is more a learning to see God. You do not know how God looks as you have convinced yourself of a certain identity that God must wear.

God is not painted whatever color you wish him to be. God is God and God fills all roles and all areas of creation. So, if God is all of these things and if God is every person and thing, surely you can allow every person and thing to go about their creating without interference. See how you react when I suggest total acceptance? All of your fears rushed to the surface and you wish to have control over those who might harm you, or cause pain to you or a loved one. This is due to the fact that you misinterpret the word acceptance. I have taught you that you too are God and you must allow God to be. So, not only do you accept all as God and allow it, you accept you as God and allow you.

You may fight or you may run. All choices are yours, you get to live your life and act out your stuff, and if you don't like the effect of your actions you can change how you act to get a more loving and comfortable effect. Say someone tells you that you are awful. You may slug that person, or walk away, or run and hide, or tell them what you think, or just stand there dumbfounded. In turn, each of your responses will create another response in this person, and he may slug you back if you have chosen to slug, or he may run if you slug back, or he may stand dumbfounded. Whatever responses are in you are also in him and you may trigger any of them depending on how you are treating you at the time.

If you are running from yourself you will draw someone who runs. If you are hating yourself you will draw someone who hates. You are shadow boxing with a mirror image and each thing that you do creates a ripple effect that rolls over on to the next you, and the next, and the next. If you have ever stood with a mirror in front of you and a mirror behind you, you will see how your reflection goes on and on and there is no end to it. One after another you stand, and if one falls you all fall. This is creation. You are all connected and when one falls all are affected and when one is lifted up all are affected.

This is why I ask you to love yourself, lift yourself up and stop pushing you or your reflections down. All will go up if you go up. You can only see through your eyes and your eyes lie. They do not see things as they really are so it takes a bit of trust and faith, blind faith you might say, to get you into the groove of acceptance. It is like shifting gears, and once you are in gear it will be much easier to make the next shift up. It will also be easier to stay up.

You are moving at a very fast pace right now and you are moving into the light. This causes complications for you, as you are so accustomed to seeing darkness in everything and you really don't want to be told, that what you chose to see as darkness all your life is actually light. My pen has her own darkness and I want her to begin to see it as light. She feels used and violated and I ask Liane to see the good in all. Even what you call abuse can be good. It is all a level of perspective. Look at where she is in her growth. She *chose* sexual abuse to push her more quickly into the light and into the next dimension or reality on this plane. She is impatient for her return to God and so she chose a strong situation in hopes of being propelled into greater heights. It worked and now she must learn to see the good in her entire situation and maybe even thank those who assisted.

So, have you used others to boost you ahead in your growth and do you appreciate them for what they have done? This is the time of learning the truth and switching from dark to light, and the ability to do so is already in you. *Look for the good!* It is there and it has always been working for you and not against you. God has always been you; you just haven't been looking for God, as you were so busy seeing evil. Let go of evil, it is not yours to keep. Switch over to God and know that God is good, and everything is God so everything is good.

⚜

You are now at a time in your existence where you will transform. Transformation is done gradually and with care. It may feel like you are being stretched and pulled, and you are. You are being molded and shaped and worked over as with clay. When you begin to sculpt a beautiful creation you begin with an "idea" and create from there. As you go you may find it necessary to change small details or even large details. It is all part of this process of creation.

You will find that, in creating your own God-self, you may choose to change as you go. Change is good and it is also what is. Change is spontaneity. Every occurrence is spontaneously created and brought to life. This creates great turmoil for those who have great fear of moving into an unknown future or an unknown creation. Most of what you already know is safe for you, only because you know it. If you do not know your future you feel unsafe. If you have projected into a future, you feel safe. If you have no idea what the future holds for you, you feel traumatized and often paralyzed in your fear.

You are so afraid of an uncertain future because you do not trust you. You think you are awful and you think you are incompetent to create good for yourself. Even if you were to create good, you will soon find something wrong with that so that you may call it bad or awful. You do this out of habit. You are so accustomed to seeing bad and watching for bad that you can now turn anything into bad.

We are going to change you. We are going to turn everything you see into good and this will become your new habit. I will show you how to look for the good and you will enjoy learning how to turn darkness into light. We are now going to have our first lesson. You are going to move out into your day and see absolutely everything that occurs as a good thing. If someone slugs you I want you to think, "Oh good, I needed to know that I can get hit and still live;" or, "Oh good, I needed to know how this person really is;" or, "Oh good, I'm finally getting my revenge on myself for being stupid about life." I don't care how silly you get with your reasoning, but do find good.

It will help you to know that you must let go of all preconceived ideas to become God; so you may as well start by letting go of the idea that you may be learning something bad, by teaching yourself to see good in a situation you currently label bad. You will learn as you go that there are no bad choices and there are no bad situations.

❀

As you begin to notice your own inability to love your own self, you will begin to allow you more time to heal your wounds – wounds that were brought on by you in order to hide part of you or maybe to cut off part of you. These type wounds do not heal if ignored. They do heal when you open the door and allow them some light.

You are in a position to heal all parts of you just by being you. You may begin to accept you and by doing so you allow the light to shine on all parts of you. You will see that, in acceptance, you find light and love. You will tune into the light and let go of your hold on judgment. As you do so you will find that you not only do not rush into judgment, you do not wish revenge. Revenge is when you strike out in some way, or maybe your way to get back or even with someone is simply to "do unto them as they have done unto you."

Usually you go for "a hurt for a hurt." You know how to punish them and you know how to upset them or push them into their fear and this is how you control one another. You may not speak with the one who has hurt you in a move to get revenge, as you know how this person fears rejection. Your idea is to give them what they fear to get even for what they did to you. In the end this works out for all involved, as you all fear losing and this is a way to put you in a position where you *believe* that you have lost. In actuality you have both won, as good is in everything and both parties know this on some level, and so this is the game you play.

It will help you to know that each time you play this revenge game you learn a little bit more about yourself, as you are the one you are actually seeking revenge on. You are all there is and the rest that you see are your reflections. So, each time you seek to hurt back, you are hurting you or pushing at your own fear buttons. I just thought you would like to know.

So; it is totally up to you. You control the reflections by your initial action. You may fight or you may love. You are fighting you and loving you. You may "take away from" or "give to" and it has nothing to do with anything but you. You fight you and you love you. You may make life easy on yourself or you may make life tough. It's all up to you and it's all your choice. *You are the creator!*

As you learn to create from love you will learn to love. Loving is spontaneous and loving feels very, very good. It does not hurt and you do not hurt the one you love. You have simply chosen to act out on someone who reminds you most of you. Look at how you feel toward your mate or close friend and you will know how you feel toward you. You treat those closest to you as you would treat your own self. You are most connected to them and your *idea* of your identity is spread out to them. You actually begin to tell them how to act and look at life, and even how to dress. This is you taking over because you do not wish to be you. You are looking for a way out of you and you use someone else to live through.

If you see someone who is clinging to you for dear life and is always around no matter how often you push them away, this person too is searching for someone else to fulfill his or her needs. The needs are great and he or she is not willing to take responsibility for his or her life. You all do this. You each play a "hurt me" or "I am hurt" role. Victim/victimizer. It is the game you play. Good guy/bad guy. Now this game is being exposed because it is no longer advantageous for you to pretend to be what you are not.

How can you be the victim of death when death is a beautiful doorway to the other side or to the light? Does this make you a loser or a winner? How can you be a victim of rape when this event will allow you the opportunity to face your own fears regarding your body and your identity, and in this process you may project into an entirely new perspective and raise your level of wisdom and enlightenment? Is this then victimization or is it winning? You are very confused due to judgment and I will allow you the time necessary to *discharge* this false idea from your bodies and minds. Good does not really exist and neither does bad. Creation exists and creation is nothing more than "becoming God."

For the most part you are learning the process of becoming. You are learning to be you and what you are. You are learning to be love. Love is not misunderstood so much as it is totally absent. Love is the knowledge and awareness that allows for acceptance. With love you will find your own center and your own trust in yourself. You are moving toward a time of total light. There will be a movement toward light and it will be big. It will be so big that you may begin to fear the light as it may feel a little overwhelming for you.

You will not learn about the light by not moving out of the dark. If you stay in the dark you see dark. As you begin to move out of your own darkness, you will begin to see that you are indeed moving into an entirely new identity. You will become the best of you. You will become so strong in your faith in yourself, that you will know you are creating absolutely everything you see. You are creating from balance and not from distorted truth that says you are evil. You will be creating from a very loving place and all will feel good as you will see only good.

You will become such a free shining beam of light that you will fill you up with light. You will feel brand new and without fear of your future. You will be as a child, starting out again with no preconceived ideas that shout out "danger" and "warning" at every turn. You will learn to allow your experiences to teach you joy, and you will allow yourself to receive joy. As you move into this new state you will not be affected by what you call negative, as all negative will be washed away by the light and you will be left seeing only the good in every situation.

You will begin to take part in creation with full knowledge that you are the creator as well as the creation. You will know that you wrote this script of your life for a very good reason and you will know that you can do rewrites at any time. For the first time in creation you will be taking an active part in the creating with full awareness that it is all you. You will not get upset with your reflections and you will not get upset with you. You will know that the purpose is to grow to a higher awareness and that what you learn as you grow will be most valuable in getting you higher.

You are spinning up and you are turning to light particles. This is ascension. You are in it now and have been for some time. You are so powerful in your force of creation that you may spin up or spin down. You make this transition out of a free will choice and you choose as you see best for your own evolution. So; if you each do this, how can anyone possibly be on the wrong track? Everyone is exactly where they need to be every second of every day. You are you and they are themselves. You let them create as they see fit and they (as your reflection) will let you create as you see fit.

Life is no more than a series of choices, and if you constantly try to force your choices on others you are not *allowing* all possibilities. You are here to learn to become God. The funny part is that you already are God and you already know all. You just went off to dreamland so you could create fantasy lands, and now you are so preoccupied with your fantasy that you forgot your name. You are God.

You are universal intelligence. You are "the Light."

&&&

As long as we are all one we might as well begin to act like we are. So, what does all one mean? All one is not necessarily individual without regard to difference. All one could be many things. It could be all one nation, all one culture, all one belief system or all one perspective. It could also be all one person, whole and individual and united. All one could be a connection between good and bad, love and hate. Meaning love actually is all there is, so hate is part of love or a different view of love. Good is all there is, so bad is simply a different view of good. It is equal energy brought out and twisted to mean something different or opposite.

So; if you are all one, maybe you are all one soul bringing forth a different energy and twisting it to make it bend as you wish. Maybe all are exactly the same identity and only *perceive* a difference out of creative response to be in matter. After all, you did come here to create and to make more of yourself. So if created matter is simply energy and you are simply energy, why are you different or individual from other living and nonliving things? You are not. You are no more and no less important than a rock.

I just thought you might like to know that you too are rocks in that you too are simply created form out of energy. A rock has little to say and, of course, we can't seem to shut you up, but basically you are one. This is what I want you to remember as you go about your day today. It will help you ease your responsibility load concerning choices. You may sit and be quiet as a rock or you may hustle and bustle about and create conflict and excitement. You are no more valuable to God than a rock. Why? Because God is the rock and God is you. You are God and rocks are God. All one! Everyone and everything are all one. This is your thought for today.

❧

As we become God, we will be as little or as big as we wish. We will be only as big as we believe and only as small as we believe. So, if you are in control of who and what you are simply by how you believe, then I suggest you create you exactly the way that you want to be.

You will find that you are as large and as grandiose as you choose to be. You are also as small and insignificant as you choose to be. It all has to do with power to create and how you *use* your power to create. You may virtually have it all or you may have nothing. This choice is yours and always has been. As you grow in power you will begin to see how you effectively create in your life. You will see how you simply have to change your perception in order to create something new. This, of course, is due to the fact that light attracts light and dark attracts dark. When you create from light you get more light. When you create from fear or dark you get more dark.

So; as you go along you will wish to be aware and begin to create only from love. Of course, if you still wish to grow and learn regarding dark areas in you, you may choose to create from dark. It is up to you and it really has no consequence in the total picture. It is more to do with how you "play" your hand. You may draw new cards or you may fold. You may raise the bet or you may drop out of this game altogether. You are in control and it is up to you. *Free will* is your greatest gift. Use it wisely and know that it is not meant to be handed over at every turn to someone else. It is not for others to make your choices and it is not for you to make their choices.

Free will is yours to use for you and free will is theirs to use for them. Allow them to live their own lives as they see fit and do not suggest that they change or even accept your ways. Allow them to be who they are. If you suggest they change and they do, it has little to do with you and everything to do with them. Tend your own garden. Clean out your own weeds and harvest your own fruit. Do it for you. Do it alone, out of great love. Be you alone. No one else on this plane has the right to be you. You are you and you may control you, or shoot you, or love you, or hate you. No one may do for you, as only you are you. When and if you choose to die, who will be laying in your coffin, them or you?

Live your entire life for you, as you are the only one you can live for. You came into life alone and will go out alone. You are a gift to you. Use your gift wisely. You are the only you there is in all of creation. You belong to you and no one can ever take you away. You may continue to push yourself away and reject yourself and try to get others to take responsibility for you, but the bottom line is that you cannot get rid of you. You cannot simply turn your soul over to another. The good news is that you may love you and cherish you and change anything about you at any given moment. You are completely and totally in charge of you. Take real good care of you....

As we move into the future we will do so with a sense of accomplishment. We will know that we are the creator and we will know that we have been creating for some time out of lack (deficiency). We will know that with awareness we may change our creativeness into light. Our awareness grows as we grow, and to be aware of your own power is a very good thing.

You created your entire life centered around power. Many of you chose not to use your power, as you felt you were abusive in the past and power was best left to others. Those of you who chose to ignore power in life will more than likely be playing some level of victim role. You put aside your power in order to see how you could create without it. You actually fear your own power in many instances and you do not trust yourself to use it wisely. Have you ever heard someone say, "Oh, that's too much for me – I don't need that much money?" Or maybe it's an authoritarian position that is too much for you, "No. Don't put me in charge; I don't want to tell people what to do." Usually you do, but you are afraid to have power over others out of fear of your own inability in the past to deal with power.

Many of you have been the kings and queens and land barons, or maybe you were simply a thug or marauder. Maybe you have used others for the fun of it, so now you are playing the opposite roll out of fear of doing it again. The belief that is very strong among you is, "Do unto others as you would have done unto yourself." So, as you go out of life and return in a new life you choose to "do unto yourself before you do unto others again." This is how you control your emotional body. You punish you for your own sins and you nail you to a cross so you will not commit the same crime again.

This brings us to "trust." You must learn to trust that you are God and you are creating for God. You must let go of this need to punish yourself for past discretions. You must allow you to be. You must begin to know who you are and what makes you tick, and this will allow you to trust your own motives and your own behavior. Once you know how to trust you, you will allow yourself power to create on a very big scale. Power is good, it is not bad. Power is what you are. Do not deny what you are. You are the most powerful God Almighty. How can you fear what you are?

As you go along in your day today, I wish you to remember that you are here to learn to love you. There is no other reason. When you love you, you will raise up and ascend. Love you and you will be God. God is here and it is only his own ignorance that blocks his view of himself. Can you see the God in you? Are you aware that you are God? Can you trust you? Do you know you? And do you love what you are?

So far it is not difficult to see how you fear. You fear love and you fear life and you 'fear' fear. You have always been in a position to love and now is the time. I wish you to love all that you are. Love all parts of you and know that all parts of you are tolerable. Not only are you tolerable, you are lovable. Do you know that you need not change to be loved by God? Do you know that you are loved as you are? Do you know that you are God learning to love God? Do you know that you judge God as imperfect and unlovable?

How can this be? How can you be so confused as to know what is not the truth and to not know what is most eminently the truth? How is it that you cannot accept you and love you as you are? By the way, you do know by now that if you cannot accept you and love you as you are, you will not be allowed to accept others as lovers as they are. It is simply your reflection. You can only give to them what you *allow* yourself to give to you.

So; if you find that in your relationships, you are not comfortable or are not accepting; it is due to the fact that you cannot get comfortable with you. You do not allow you to accept you as you are, so how can you possibly expect yourself to accept others without wanting to improve upon their low-life-intelligence? This is what you deal with in all of your relationships. You deal with you and how you want to change you and fix you and I want you to simply learn to *accept* you. And in accepting you, you will begin to accept all that occurs in your life with grace and with charm. This is what is known as a "charmed" life.

You are meant to be charming and you are meant to be lovable. You are not meant to be anything less than perfect. As you go about your life, I wish you to remember that not only are you responsible for you... you are a gift to you! You are a present bestowed on you and you must learn to take good care of you, and love you, and cherish you. You will find that in loving you, you are loving all that is, for you are all that is. You are the creative force who is God. Love you, cherish you. Know who you really are.

For as long as you have been here you have both loved and revered God. The only problem is that you did not know God. You never took the time to figure out who God was or how God came to be. You only accepted that there was something more powerful than you. Sometimes it was the wind you revered, and so you had your Wind God and you had your Fire God and your Earth God. It is all you, you know? All gods are you and all the power comes from you.

You will find that as you learn about your own pain you will see pain everywhere, and as you learn about your own joy you will see joy everywhere. What you see is simply what your focus is on. You may watch your news and not notice or have a reaction to the news. Then at other times you are totally consumed and overwhelmed by it. You call it "getting *into* it" and this is exactly what it is. When you are liking it and "into it" you have a good ol' time with it. When you are not interested you are simply not "into it."

This is a literal connotation. You are "into it" or you are "*out* of it." It is as you focus your attention that you go "into" or "out of" focus. You focus on what you are. If you are working on the lesson of forgiveness you will begin to see many situations where people are easily forgiving and forgetting, or you will see those who are harboring ill will toward others. Either way, it is you focusing on what you are going through within. It is your current state of internal affairs being projected forward to be viewed on your movie screen.

As you learn to uncover bigger and bigger disturbances you may begin to focus on bigger and bigger disturbances. You will always get what you are and you always are what you get. So, as you go about your day, I wish you to begin to know that it is all you and it has nothing to do with anyone you are focusing on.

❧

You are not here to learn to become all one. You are here to learn to be an expression of God. You are not all the same expression. It is as though you are his dialect. He has spoken to you and you are his ability to express in a certain style or manner. Be you. Be *your* own individual expression. It is not necessary to all think alike or speak alike. Allow diversity. Allow differences. It is glorious to see the various species of nature. The plant and animal kingdom do not force change on those they encounter. They simply move on and allow others to nest or roam and survive or not survive. It is okay to allow everyone and everything to be or not be, to destroy itself or not destroy itself. You are too concerned about how others live and I wish you to focus only on you. You will see that you are not so much afraid to be who you are as you are afraid to come out of denial of what you are.

Denial is great and it was painted in place long ago. Denial is the facade, the false front, the part of you that you pull down to shut out the world when you are most afraid. Denial is the part of you that you use to protect you from the truth, because you fear the truth most of all.

Denial will tell you when you are not good, or when you are being bad. Denial believes strongly in good vs. bad. Denial is the part of you that is rejection. The part of you that is rejection will always reject anything that does not feel safe. This part of you has great fear and no trust. If you allow denial, you will find yourself locked up behind the walls you built to protect you from your own emotions.

Denial is the part of you that will allow you only what feels good and safe to you. And what feels good and safe? Your return to pain. If you were hurt you will return to hurt. If it is connected to childhood and the child believes, "bad things happen to me because I am bad," that part of you will feel safe around certain individuals. And most often a sense of safety is tied to the knowledge that these certain individuals may strike out in some way and give you pain. Some part of you feels very comfortable with pain.

Remember in our earlier books, I cautioned you to seek out those who make you a little uncomfortable? Seek out those who are not what you feel most comfortable with. They will give you what you are not seeking. They will give you joy instead of pain. You are all seeking a return to the nest and yet the nest is what you most fear. You are better off to *risk*. Change your programming and risk pure joy without denial of it. Risk being unsafe and uncertain in your relationships. You will find that you will feel most safe and most comfortable with those who are *like* you in some way. So, if you carry great pain and the ability to create pain, they will carry great pain and the ability to create pain.

Break your addiction to pain. Make your own joy

by not denying who you are and how you create for yourself. You may draw whomever you like into your life and you may make whatever choices you wish. It is good to know yourself thoroughly, then you may recognize your own denial of good within your choices.

As you go about making choices, I highly suggest you let go of your need to punish yourself for past deeds. This part of you is way out of control, and you have hung yourself on the cross long enough. It's time to see joy where you once saw misery. Can you be comfortable with joy? Can you accept joy? Can you live in joy? In order to experience joy you must let go of your need for safety. Safe to you is what you are comfortable with, and what you are comfortable with is the coat you have always worn. It is a coat of thorns, and now to take it away from you will make you scream. So I will allow you to remove your old, comfortable coat of thorns and I will be waiting with your new coat of soft, fuzzy fleece. It will take a little adjusting, but you will find it much more comfortable in the long run.

As you return from denial you will sense that you have been cheated. You want to get even or get revenge on those who taught you about pain. Revenge will create more pain, so I suggest you let it go. The best way to handle those who *you believe* have caused you pain in the past, is to accept that you had an agreement with them in order for you to learn to evolve, and then you let them go. You need not hold on to a match after it has done its job and lit your candle for you. If you do not require further service from your match "let it go." You need not hold on to anyone or anything. It is simply not necessary. Move on and know that you will always draw to you exactly what you need at every moment of every day.

You will find that as you learn to let go of denial you will wish to be free to *accept*. Accepting is the opposite of denying and accepting has no "push," no "resistance" and therefore no "pain." No pain-- a pain-free existence is waiting for you. Come out of denial and accept what is waiting for you. You do deserve it all. You are not being punished by a mean God who sits in heaven and judges over you. You are being punished by you and your own addiction to a need for pain. Let it go. Let go of the chaos you create for yourself. It is no longer necessary. You are good now and you know it.

❦

*A*s you begin to see who you are you will wish to *judge* what you see. This is actually considered a natural reaction since you live with great confusion concerning what is right and what is wrong. You are moving into a situation where you are best to not judge and not condemn yourself. Leave you alone! Allow your truth to be and do not judge you for acting or responding to trapped emotions.

As your trapped feelings begin to surface do not justify nor deny them. Simply allow you to be by vibrating and *releasing* your hold on strong emotional pain. Speak your truth if you must in order to release these trapped feelings. This is part of coming out of denial and facing the fact that you have emotional trauma trapped in your mind. Once you have released your emotional baggage it will no longer *control* your life. You will be free to experience love and joy and no longer feel trapped in pain and denial.

All denial is self-denial and it is blocking you or denying you your own good. You are here to receive your good not to deny it. You will begin by allowing you to have feelings and emotions. All feelings are meant to move, as all energy is meant to move. Allow your feelings to be. You may experience anger or revenge or hate. These are feelings and they must not be *stuffed* down in you or you will explode from too much trapped energy. You will bloat up or throw up or simply drop dead from an attack on you by your own pain. You will call this a heart attack or an asthma attack or a virus of some sort attacking you, but it is all your own feeble attempt to hide or deny your own feelings.

As you begin to uncover more and more of you, you may actually frighten yourself by some of your own un-manifested emotional energy. You have stuff plugging you up that has been in you for eons, and when it comes out you may find yourself wanting to deny that these feelings could have anything to do with you. You will want to push them away from you, and this takes us back to Book Four and the story of God separating himself by pushing at what he began to *feel* moving within his own beingness.

This is the original separation of Father/Mother

God. This is the original separation of twin souls or negative/positive energy. You are at denial, which is connected to the original fall of consciousness into unconsciousness, or darkness. You are at the part of you that will reveal your true essence once you *allow* it to balance. Do not be afraid of you. Do not push you away from you. Learn to trust that you are all things and that all things serve a higher purpose.

You will find that as you allow all feeling to be, you will be. You are your feelings. Your thoughts and emotions are you. You control them as they move through you. Do not fear this part of you. Trust that you will create from wisdom and clarity once you come into balance on your polarities. You are opposite ends of the same stick and this confuses you, because you think you can only focus on the good end, or what you think is the good end. You focus on each end and everything in the middle, but because you have separated yourself you cannot see what the other you's are focusing on.

Now it's time to come together *within you*. You will learn to focus on all possibilities and to see all positions at once. This will allow you the freedom of a greater selection of possibilities to create from. Once you have learned to create from all angles, you will know independence from limitation. You are no longer a limited being. You are becoming unlimited.

You have become what you feel and you are afraid of your own feelings. Feelings are part of your circuitry and you will learn to allow them their place. All feelings are in you for a reason. You will not succeed by running from who you are. You will get ahead by acknowledging who you are and the energy you carry. You are the one who chose to experience feeling on this plane. It is part of the draw to this level of creation.

You experience emotional outlet and then your feelings regarding your movement of the emotions come into play. You are no longer creating from feelings of fear and so you must trust your own emotions. This is upsetting to most of you who have buried your emotions. You said, "I don't have to look at this and I will not accept it as mine." You do have to look if it is part of you or you will be denying part of you. You will find that as these buried emotions begin to surface you may have conflict and ill will toward those you feel unsafe being around. If you feel threatened I suggest you find a release or this threat will push you into an explosion of emotional response. It is best to find someone you can safely speak with, who will not judge you nor those you feel threatened by.

Allow yourself the time that is necessary to rebuild a strong emotional foundation. You will find that it is not so difficult as you believe. You have already begun the groundwork and most of what you are experiencing now is the *shift* over to a new, brighter perspective. You are literally being created as you go. You are *becoming* and you are in your transformation process. You will find that after a time you will begin to feel from a new perspective and you will begin to know that you are God.

It is difficult to tell you how wonderful you will feel as you have no perception at this time of such a high level of enjoyment. As you move deeper into your own discord you actually create beauty just by looking and accepting. The feelings will be allowed movement and this will allow you to live and not die. This is the final step in "becoming." The movement of energy into the field of spirit will bring spirit in touch with feeling and feeling in touch with spirit. This is the melding of God and man. Do not be afraid when you begin to feel.

⊰⊱

When you begin to become aware that you carry hostile energy, you will become aware that you are more than you care to know. You actually have this ability to harm and this frightens you. You actually have the ability to be a villain, and since you all judge villains you do not wish to be on the villain end of this good guy/bad guy game that you play. You are all the same. I do not care if you are a saint, you still have the ability to kill or maim and this frightens you. The energy that you carry within yourself frightens you and you are therefore afraid of your own self.

You are afraid to be you and you are afraid to not be you. You do not know how to deal with you, because you have not actually discovered all parts of you and you are afraid that some parts may be activated without your conscious consent.

You are not going to explode from being you. You may, however, explode from denying you and not wanting to accept who and what you are. You are not so much in danger of exploding and killing another as you are in danger of imploding and killing you. You are seeing this type of behavioral effect every day. Some implode and die of "attack" by their heart or cancer cells or lung congestion, while others simply go out and start shooting at everyone and everything that they see. It is all the same energy. It is death by denial of one's own true nature. *Learn to accept you.* You are not bad. Do not judge your feelings and urges as bad. Learn to allow movement of these feelings.

Movement is not necessarily acted on. Because you know you have hatred does not mean you will go out and kill. Knowledge is simply awareness, and awareness will allow you to direct your energies into more productive channels. Knowledge and awareness give you opportunities you do not have if you continue to stay hidden in denial. You must come out of denial and look at what you are so angry about. If you deny that you have anger you are in direct denial. *All* have anger as anger is part of all... you saints will find that you too carry this energy and sometimes manifest it in your lives as a strong belief in right and wrong. In such cases, you are using your anger to control your emotions and it is killing you as surely as it kills those who act out anger.

So, let's stop all this nonsense about good people and bad people. Good people are bad and bad people are good. Everyone is everything because everything is all there is. In actuality nothing is, but you are not that far in your evolution yet. So, for now, simply know who you are and how you tick like a bomb from not being your true self. This is what kills you. This is what ages you and this is what death is. Death is belief that part of you is not acceptable, so you try to shut off that part of you in order to be lovable and acceptable. In doing so you have lost touch with love, and this is due to the fact that you cannot love if you are not love.

✣

*A*s you begin to reach a level of awareness that allows you to see how you often do not accept your own good, you will see how parts of you are blocking you from receiving. You will see how you no longer have full control over what you have created for yourself and you are afraid you will never have control. Most often you are in a position of receiving and then you don't. You simply turn your back and decide not to risk and say, "It is best this way." Then you feel very sad but also very "on top" of things, as you did not allow something to occur that may have frightened you.

It may be as simple as a job offer that you turn down in order to be with your family, or it may be a relationship you let go of in order to keep your career. If it was the job offer, you probably convinced yourself that you were being good and right to stay where your family wanted you to stay. This is giving others say over what your wishes are. This is a way of giving your good away for righteous reasons. If it were the relationship you let go of because your job is your way of taking good care of you, then you again did it out of fear. Fear that you could not have another job in another location with this particular person, or fear that this person is too much for you to handle and you are too insecure to risk losing a job over a relationship.

So; how do you choose and which is the right and good choice? You will find that in every choice you make, you will be battling with you. The less fear you have regarding the situation, the smaller the battle. Everything is simply a choice and every choice carries a gift. If you are good at creating pain to punish yourself for past sins, you will be good at finding bad in even the best situation.

You will learn that, as you move out of your own darkness and fear, you have no place to go but to the light. You are moving in that direction now and as you get fully into the light you may begin to see more darkness. This is due to the fact that as you come out of the dark into the light, you actually expose the parts of you that are darkest, and, in the light, they appear even darker by contrast. So, don't worry too much about how the world is suffering and falling apart. I have an excellent view from here, and from what I see life is great, you are loved, and the world is in very good hands.

Don't be so afraid of making the wrong choice. There are no wrong choices and you can't do the wrong thing for yourself. Learn to love yourself above all else and you will raise yourself above all else. This is how you will find that creating does not take control, creating only takes thought – beautiful thoughts create beautiful creations. Happy creating my beautiful friends.

So far it is not acceptable to be who you are. Your behavior is all wrong and you seem to judge yourself at every turn. This, of course, is due to the fact that you no longer allow yourself freedom. You are so afraid of freedom that you actually control yourself and manipulate yourself at all times. This is the part of you that is in charge and wants you to be accepted by those you believe to be better than you are. Why are you believing them to be better? Because you do not live *in* them, you live in you. You believe that you are at a certain level of respectability and acceptability, and you wish to avoid being judged by anyone who believes they are above you on this scale you have created.

So, who is more lovable and acceptable, a man who

is fat and bald and has a wart on the end of his nose or a man who is tall, dark and handsome? Who is more acceptable and which one will make you stand up straighter and adjust your tie or your hair if you have an interview for a job? Who gets you to take notice of your own disarrayed appearance? Are you intimidated by those who dress well and look attractive, or are you intimidated by those who are unattractive in physical form? Do you wish to get to know those who dress well and look good, or do you wish to get to know those who dress a little off-beat and don't bathe quite so often?

Are you afraid of being alone on a street corner with certain types, or looks that are different than you are accustomed to? You are all judging one another on how you dress and look and act. So what? It is okay to judge. Now I have really done it, all of this yapping through eleven books about not judging and now I say, "So what;" it's your business, it's your *choice*; it's your free *will* to do whatever you please and whenever you please. Judge away. Have a good time creating and changing your mind and growing and evolving.

I don't care if you judge and I do not judge you for it. *Nothing* is wrong in the eyes of God and, since *you* are *becoming* God, you had best get used to the role. You are allowed to be who you are. Be any way that you wish, as you may always find fault if you look for it. You may also find good if you look. You are working with a two-sided coin and you may toss it one year to find that it falls on its "head" and that makes "tales" the winning game that year. The next year you may toss this same coin to find it lands on its "tail" and makes "heads" the winning game.

So; are you out when "tales" is in or are you out when "heads" is in? This is the game you play with yourself. It is called good and bad, right and wrong; and you are so addicted to this game that you are like a gambler who has lost his car and his home and he still will not quit. I tell you now that you will break these habits and you will rise above your addictions and needs. Right now we will start with judgment. I have used it to teach you because it works, and you love to outdo yourself with your own theorizing of how you must not do this or how you must do that, which is in itself a judgment, but you love it so I use it.

Now, don't get all upset and jump into your ego here. This is a lesson in rising above judgment which literally means that judgment does not exist from a higher level, so what does it matter if you do something that doesn't even exist? You figure this out while I have a talk with Liane about our plans for tomorrow.

❧

You are now in a position to know light. You have always wanted to know the truth and now you are learning and growing with the truth. The truth is many, many things. As you begin to work out your own truth you will discover that you are a product of many areas of creation.

You are primarily a product of solidity and density and you are changing daily into a product of light.

As you begin to grow in light you take on certain characteristics. One of these may be physical change. You may begin to see your body breakdown in certain ways and this is the disintegration of matter. It is the breakdown of the densest forms within. You are beginning to reform you without death and a new birth. You are breaking down what is solid in order to create a light body. As you begin to see subtle changes take place within the body, you will feel subtle changes take place within the emotions. These are being transformed also. As you move into the light, you will find greater opportunities for growth and greater choices based on awareness.

As you move toward this new emotional state, you will find that your moods may shift drastically and you may run from hot to cold. You may be excitable one minute and simply not care the next. You may want to move to China one day and decide to stay home the next. You will be running energy up and down the newly discovered areas of perception and when you begin to perceive from all points of view, you have a much broader spectrum to create from.

So, don't think you are going crazy; you are simply going to the light and testing out your newly formed frequencies. You are gradually moving *up* the scale and it will be best to allow this process without judging it as undesirable. You are going to find that you will be able to be many things when you let go of your attachment that you must be one way or another. You will discover that not only do you begin to rise in this process, you also begin to expand. You literally become more of what you are. And as you become more of what you are it is easier for you to see what you want. It's sort of like putting you under a giant magnifying glass to look at all parts of you.

So; as these parts become visible to you, through this wondrous process of ascension, I wish you to accept all of you without punishment and without disgust. Just say, "Okay, this is me and I am quite a unique creation. Would you look at that!" Something along these lines will do. You may wish to keep your newfound self to yourself, until you can adjust to knowing these new parts and accepting them as you.

You are very easily misguided by others and this is why it is best to save some of you just for you. I know you are taught to share on earth, but this too is a misconception of your own making. Be you and keep you. You are the keeper and caretaker of you and it is no longer necessary to ask another how you should handle responsibility for your own care. God will guide you from within. Others are guided for their own path and you will be guided along yours. Often when you listen to others, you end up walking in their shoes instead of your own.

So; allow for the shifting of emotions and allow for the change within the body structure as well. You are all changing and growing in various ways and not all will experience the same changes at the same time. It depends on where you are in the energy cycle that spins you around this dense plane. If you are meant to change and grow at certain times of the year, you will feel this as a troubled and uncomfortable time. Then it may pass and you won't feel growing pains until next year around this time. Everything circles everything else. This is nature and you are part of nature.

I will leave you with this advice; do not become so totally absorbed in your own growth that you begin to assume that those around you are not growing right along with you. They are! All are evolving at this time. It is impossible to be on the earth and not evolve with it. Those who choose to not evolve will simply leave as you are seeing many do. This is okay to. All ways are acceptable... right?

⁂

As long as you continue to find fault with yourself you will continue to not love yourself. I want you to begin to love you by accepting you, and the only way to do this is by accepting all that you have done. All that you have done is pretty broad in that you have created every crime and disgrace imaginable in the past lives you have shared with others. You kill, you rob, you pillage and plunder and rape and burn at the stake, and hang people and commit suicide and any other offensive act that you cannot accept.

Do you not see how in pushing these things away as bad, awful and horrifying, you are pushing that part of you that remembers into denial? It will not be allowed to be who it is, as it is composed of offensive behavior. You must forgive you. Now is the time for forgiveness and openness and allowing you to come forward into the light. What do you think moving into the light is? It is saying, "Okay I accept, I love you" to all parts of you. You must learn to love all of you and stop judging any part of you as not lovable. You will rise so much faster if you can accept that you are all and all is you.

You do not need to do any act of contrition for your offenses. Simply let them be acceptable behavior in the long, drawn out process of birthing God. How can you not wish to accept everything that is part of God? God is in you. You are in God. God does no wrong in creating. Creation is the process of becoming and expanding and growing. How can expansion into certain areas of creation ever be considered bad? How can you turn energy into something it is not? How can you allow you to be heads but not tales? You are both sides of this coin. Do not shut part of God out simply because you do not understand the reasoning behind creation. You are in no position to judge. You can only see a pinpoint of the light at this time and you have no idea how vast the entire scope of reality is.

It is best not to get too involved in self righteous behavior until you are more aware of the entire picture. You know so little and you see even less. You must learn to broaden your view of humanity and this will broaden your scope of loving awareness. You are most interested in love as you have been called to wake up to what you are, and what you are is love.

So; as you go about your day, I wish you to judge

no one and nothing (since you love to be told what to do and how to do it). This will assist you in seeing how everything that ever occurs may be perceived as good if you will only *allow* it to. See, you are the creator of your reality and if you just allow it, it can be. You have full control of your creation and when you are tired of running your old, hurtful, pain-filled movies you will tune in to love and acceptance and allow yourself and everyone else the gift of forgiveness.

☙❧

*A*s long as you continue to reject parts of you, you will continue to experience rejection. It is most likely "how you are treated" that shows you how you treat you. So, I do suggest that you begin to love all parts of you and no longer push these parts away. Judgment will allow you to push at all parts without concern for who you are. Without judgment you are free to be un-judged and un-guilty. Without judgment you are free to be innocent. You may wish to continue to judge and to ride deeper into the realms of judging, or you may wish to rise above judgment as a matter of survival.

You will find that judging is based on taste and choice and to judge is not bad. It is a choice and it is also a pushing at part of you that does not wish to play the role that you have assigned it to play. You do not always judge when you make choices. Often you make a choice based on desire and this is how you learn what you want and don't want.

When you learn how to choose without using judgment you will be choosing from option rather than choosing from the principles of good vs. bad. You will find that you can just as easily go one way as you can the other. You will find that you are more afraid to judge than you believe. Often you will be in a position of great wealth so you do not have to struggle with your choices as you do when you are dealing with survival issues. You are most likely to struggle with new issues once you have your desired wealth, only because you enjoy struggle. You will not clear your fear of non-survival by "having it all" and never worrying about how you will live or eat.

Maybe those of you who do not know where your next dime is coming from are in a much better position to slough off fear than those who stay cozy and safe behind wealth. Maybe what you see as security is actually a camouflage to keep you numb to the painful memories you carry regarding survival issues. Maybe you are being put in a position of survival struggle at this time and maybe, just maybe, it is a very big gift for your soul.

You decide. Don't judge it but allow it, accept it and work within it. Allow yourself the time that is necessary to experience the fear that is attached to losing a home or losing a job. Allow yourself to know that this is growth and allow yourself permission to experience this growth and get everything you can out of it.

≈♨≈

$\int$o far you have done well to stay balanced. You are not so sure of who you are or what is happening, but you are still living and breathing, so you have stayed somewhat balanced. When you decide to ascend you will learn to change your energy and to ask for the truth. The truth is very definitely going to be hard to swallow for some of you. You will find it most difficult if you have been in a severe state of denial. The greater your denial the more upsetting the truth will be.

You who are in a state of denial regarding creation are going to find it quite difficult being the creator if you have always blamed someone else for creation. Those who find the truth hardest to take will be those who have harsh judgments against themselves. This is due to the fact that judgment is not at the crux of the problem, but it is the cause. It is one of the ways in which you have offset denial. You have allowed denial to reign by allowing judgment to control your view of reality. Reality is not viewed through your eyes but through your mind.

You create your own reality and you may change what you have previously created. We do this by changing how you perceive what you have been judging. For example, if I can get you to drop judgment against death, we now have a new perception of death with less judgment and fear. This leads to all kinds of new possibilities and ways of viewing life as well as death. This is an attitude adjustment in that we are clearing old programming that says, "To die is bad and awful" and we are replacing this old programming with something "lighter" that says, "This is something good and wonderful just as all is."

Now you have a perception shift which is accompanied by an "attitude" that is lighter and filled with hope. Now the *thought* towards death is, "Oh boy, maybe there's something good here after all." Now we have a whole new view of life with death as a possible expansion, where prior to this our belief was, "Oh God, this is the end and I know it will hurt!" You are simply shifting and changing and making room for lighter possibilities. This will occur in every area of your life and you will be a little upset as you get to face each area that you judge as bad or awful. Bad and awful must open up to, "Yahoo, there's something good here after all," and you are the only one who can open these areas up for you.

You closed up and now you're going to open up to the light and truth and love. It is what you do. It is as natural as nature itself. You will learn to take on new dimensionality and become all that you were meant to be. This is just the beginning and it is how you will come back to God. As you move in this direction you may feel depressed and lost and woebegone. This is part of the process of opening up to the light. Your sorrow and depression must move to the light as well as all other areas of dark energy. We are going to move *all* of you to the light, not just the parts that you like and not just the parts that you accept. It is time to accept all and all will feel a little overwhelming until you have adjusted to this new level of awareness. It is good to hear the truth and it is good to become aware of the truth. You will also learn to trust your awareness and to move with awareness instead of fighting against it. This is good for now as I have to talk with Liane concerning sorrow.

⚜

As long as you continue to be dark dense energy you will continue to have pain. There is no pain once you move to the light. Once you give up your belief in bad, there will be no bad. Allow everything to be a gift and everything will. It is up to you how you create your own reality and it is up to you to enjoy creating and accepting your creation. It is also up to you to change what you do not enjoy by looking at it as good and enjoyable. It is most important to begin to perceive all life as a gift and to know that life is giving you exactly what is perfect for you. You may not like what you see now, but you will.

You will not necessarily change what is going on around you, but, in the shifting of your perception of what is going on around you, you are learning to see it differently. You are learning to look for the good in everything and to know that good and bad are exactly the same. There is no difference in this energy. It is only what you make of it and you seem to make of it what you most want or are addicted to. In most cases addiction overrules wants and you will change something that could be very good into something bad. This is how you present creation to yourself. If you believe you are no good you will find offense in the look of a stranger or a simple gesture that may have nothing at all to do with you. If you believe you are no good you will overhear others in conversation and turn this into "they are talking about me."

This is how you create your pain. You have the ability and the power to make any situation either good for you or bad for you. You do this on an unconscious level and it is built into your self-preservation and self-defense system. You make everything what it is by how you see it, and if you believe you are guilty of great wrongdoing in past life, or this life, you will more than likely give yourself a good dose of bad. You believe in bad and that bad deserves punishment, so you will see your life and situations in your life as bad, awful and terrible.

The best way to begin to see your life as good is to know that you are good and to know that God loves you. The quickest way to clear your addictions and imbalances within the body is to clean out the body. The best way for now is to literally wash it out. Wash out your inner tubing and allow enema a chance to heal you. You are very, very heavy inside, and enema will allow you to "lighten" your load.

As you begin to see the benefits of enema, you will also feel its effects on the physical as well as mental bodies. You will become much more open and even sensitive to what is going on in your world, your reality. You will find that, in small doses, you will begin to emerge into a new type of species who is seeing things differently and yet is not often comfortable with what you are seeing. This is all part of this transformation, and you will gradually settle into a new perspective that will add the best possible light to your particular needs.

You see, each individual is layered with past programming and each individual has his or her own way of un-layering. So to say that you know what is best for another is total nonsense, as you can only see the world through your layers and everyone else is seeing the world through their own individual layers also. So; this explains arguments and wars and different points of view. They are all here, and they all have validity, and they will all change and grow into something much broader as you change and grow into something much broader.

You are only here to shift. You came into the earth at this point in time because you wanted this jolt. You wanted to experience this great event known as transformation from matter to God. God entering matter. Light conquering dark. The peaceful existence makes its appearance on earth. God's heaven brought down to earth. The great shift. It is a very powerful time, and yes, you will feel the shift in your mental and physical and emotional and energy bodies. All parts of you are changing and adapting as quickly as possible.

You may assist you in these changes by going easy on yourself and by doing enema daily. Give yourself a break and allow yourself some off-beat, out-of-favor technique if it will help. What is the harm in putting water in your body to wash out the toxic waste that is choking your physical life out of you? You will find that as you clear your body it will even assist you in this transition. It will allow all parts of you to work together for your own good.

You are not so sure about your future as your future is being created as you go. Each step you take today directs your future, and, in some cases, changes your past. You are due for some good. Let a little "light" into your life. Allow yourself to be different and to do unique things. We are breaking old patterns, old rules and old belief systems. Your new future does not look like the past and will not be shaped from fear. Your new future is shaped from trust and faith and love, lots and lots of love.

***

It is not so difficult to see how you will not always feel good under change. You are so accustomed to living by certain rules and structure. It is most common for you to get stuck in a way of doing things and a way of thinking. This also extends into your spiritual self. You are stifled and stuck in a rut. You know the truth and yet you do not accept it readily. You are one of the few species who do not like to be free. You like restriction and boundaries and control. Freedom frightens you and you do not know how to deal with total freedom. This is due to the fact that you do not trust yourself and you judge how far you have extended yourself in previous existence.

So now you put yourself in a situation of surrender in order to find freedom within restraint. You put yourself in my hands only if I tell you to be good or to follow a set pattern. I began these books by telling you how to be love and how to let go of fear. If I had started with, "be free and do whatever you want," you would have run and tossed my writing in the trash. You are afraid to be free and do whatever you want. You are afraid to give yourself free reign as a creator. You are afraid to be responsible for you because you do not know you and you do not trust you.

Only in knowing you, will you learn to trust you. You will find it most enjoyable to finally trust who and what you are. You are not so much afraid of you as you are disappointed with yourself. You have lost hope and you have begun to struggle to survive. Hope is easily replaced and struggle will fall by the wayside once you have begun to trust your own instincts once again. It has been a very long time since you were as open to wisdom as you now are and it is not for you to judge my wisdom, it is only for you to accept it or reject it. You may do as you wish as you have free will, and free will offers you total freedom.

***

You are now in a position to be healed and this entails bringing all unhealed parts to the surface. This is how healing works. You were brought forward into the light so that light may expose all unhealed, unhealthy places in you. You are then forced to look upon your own unhealed, unhealthy garbage until you can see how you created it simply by making it garbage.

Say you have a wound on your hand and you are most perplexed as to how you received this particular wound. You may be put in a position to re-injure your hand in the same way, or a similar way, and you now remember how you did the same activity once before; therefore you surmise that this is how the initial wound took place. Now the information is planted firmly in your memory to not do this activity without care, or you might again wound yourself.

Healing is similar to this. You look at your patterns and your dysfunctional behavior, and you may repeat a trauma, or some form of turmoil, to show you how you created this particular behavior in the first place. Then you may come from a place of wisdom instead of ignorance, and you may *choose* consciously to keep the pattern or let it go. In most cases you will find it is no longer necessary to keep this outdated pattern, as most of them were meant to protect you from your own choices. Since you are now learning to trust yourself and allow all choices to be good and valuable, we can now let go of any pretense of a need for safety.

You will find that, as you grow in awareness of all your protection, you will gradually see how you have lived behind walls to keep you safe. Literally, these walls have cut you off from who and what you are. You are so busy protecting you from harm (that you believe you caused by your free will choices) that you have literally protected and kept you away from you; you who are love and light and God. Do not separate yourself from God out of fear that you will run amuck if you know how you are a spiritual being, who may or may not do as it wishes. Do not be afraid to be free to do, or not do, whatever pleases or does not please you. You are God. It is freedom that you fear. You create rule after rule and then, when you are afraid to live outside your rules, you push them at everyone else. This is your fear of God and this is how you are learning to heal.

You will no longer find it necessary to hide who you are and it will be impossible to do so. When you stand *in* the light you will see clearly how you are made up of layers of dense energy that are no longer necessary. The protection from the light must fall as the light enters. This is not a threat, this is simple fact. Light penetrates the darkness and the walls come tumbling down. This is how you will heal and, as you heal, you will fear "letting go" of your protection and you may begin to feel vulnerable and a little insecure. It is okay to be vulnerable to the light and it is okay to be insecure, as we are giving up positionality in order to see a much higher view of the total picture.

You may wish to stay hidden behind those walls of protection, but sooner or later you *will* come forward to the light, and await your turn at knocking down the walls that bind you and restrict you from receiving. In building walls you don't realize that not only would you keep out what you feared, you would also keep out love. You cannot get through to you. You are hidden behind protection, and the whole point of this series of books is to get you to drop your protection and let go of fear. If I can teach you to see it differently you will respond differently. Your entire world is created in your own mind, simply by how you perceive reality. It is not your place to accept or reject. It is your place to be, to allow yourself to be who and what you are. You are creation and you are the creator. You are playing two roles, but you are one. You are the great *I Am* who is behind and in front of everything.

Nothing and no one exists that is not you. You are everything and you control the entire world by how you perceive it. It is not so much that you shut the world down, but you shut you down, which makes it look like you have shut the world down. The world is not falling apart you are falling apart. And if you are falling apart then anything and everything you look upon will look as though it is falling apart. Begin to heal you, and as this healing takes place *in* you it will look to you as though the entire world is healing. While those who are falling apart see the world as falling apart, those who are healing will see the world as healing. You can only see from where you are. This, of course, accounts for all of those arguments and debates concerning how life is or is not.

You can never lose a debate and you can never win a debate, it simply is a controversy. This is life. Life is not one way or another. It is both ways and everything in between. When you rise up to a higher perspective you will see this. This too is a level of seeing or viewing, and once you have adjusted to viewing all perspectives you will move to the next level, which has no perspectives, or positions of negative/positive force. For now, I will leave you with this thought. You are not good or bad you simply are, and you are not male or female, you simply are.

❧

You are most forgettable when it comes to being God. You have decided to forget all of your godliness and remember only your weakness. As you begin to move into the light, these weaknesses will be exposed for what they are and you will be forced to look at the truth. The truth is that you are creating everything that you see and the truth is that you may change anything you do not like about yourself. Why allow you to be less than what you can be and why allow you to be less than you want to be?

So, as we get all of these little imperfections into perspective, you will see how you have actually used them to assist you in your growth. Now, however, we are moving into an area where it is no longer necessary to hide you from you. The truth will assist you now, where before you wanted the lies. The lies were much preferable so you did not want to give them up. It is much like a husband or wife who does not wish to acknowledge that their spouse is seeing another. It is just too painful to accept because of all the pain that is already carried in form. Now this pain is being exposed and released to allow you to move into a bright intelligent future.

You no longer need to hide the truth out of fear of taking on greater amounts of pain. You can now face the truth and see it differently. So; how do you see a husband or wife cheating as good? You might look at this and say, "Oh good, Harry is getting his needs met and I am learning that I don't own him and I am not responsible for him." Or you might look at this and say, "Oh good, Mary is off doing her thing and, to be honest, I always wanted to try that myself." There are many, many ways to be an adult and own only you. You will find that you no longer require security techniques to keep you safe from loneliness. You only require self-love, and anyone who shares anything with you, for any amount of time, is just added joy.

You need not require contracts and rules to *hold* another to you. This is the time of letting go and contracts are not part of this new you. As you move forward you will find that you no longer require anyone to stay if they wish to go, for you will be wise enough to realize that all are growing and walking their own path. You are also wise enough to know that you are not safe just because you have a mate, and you will learn to trust you and lean on you. You have been taught to lean on one another and this is what is exhausting some of you now. You are so filled with your own fears that it is difficult to add someone else's concerns to your own.

You will find that as you move along your path you will always be in your right place, and you will always find what you most need to raise you up the spiritual latter. So, if you are divorcing, do not feel bad. If you are marrying, do not feel bad. You will learn what you must and you will grow as you must. You may learn just as quickly in a marriage as you may out of marriage. You are the one who chooses your path and you are the one who will walk it.

So, if you are not happy with your choices, do not push them at another. It seems that those of you who are angry about your lot in life, want to take it out on those who made other choices that do not coincide with your choices. Do not be afraid to change your way of living and do not judge those who readily change their way of living. As far as you know, it is all good. This is your new saying for today. "It is all good."

❧

*S*o far as you know you are not too far out on a limb. You have come a long way and yet you have the option of returning home. You have been preparing for some time now and you are very, very close. When you begin this return you will find that you have forgotten a great deal regarding your true nature. You have become desensitized to the pain and addicted to the electrical charge that gives you the message that you hurt. You will find that, as you re-sensitize yourself for your return, you will pick up signals quickly and even become what many will call overly sensitive. Of course, you will not be overly sensitive, but since you have all become numb in order to sustain life, you will find sensitive to feel painful.

As you learn how to open the sensory output and input without causing the electrical jolt that says "pain," you will learn that sensitive is actually most useful. You will not only be allowed to track your emotions, you will be allowed to track the emotions of others. This is actually a form of telepathy or communication. You are beginning to *read* one another through sensory input and output. This phase of your growth will be considered painful until you get used to the idea of "feeling" what is being projected outward from another. They may say one thing, but you will read another and this is you picking up signals out of their energy field.

This works in two ways. One is that you may receive, and two is that you may send. This is done through the emotional body and is connected to all phases of your beingness. You may say, "I want you, I need you to be a part of my life," and at the same time your emotional electricity is sending out signals that say, "Do not be near me as I am afraid to get too close, for I fear that pleasure will only bring me pain." In such cases the receiver will know that you have a strong polarity in this area. He or she may translate these signals to mean that you do not find him or her desirable and so they leave.

The same is true for you. If you have said, "I want you, I need you," but your emotional body is sending the opposing signal, you may *feel* that you do not really desire this individual. We must bring your male/female, yin and yang into balance so you no longer put out mixed signals. The signal, once it is balanced within the emotional body will simply read, "I am love and I am open to love." No wants or needs will be necessary. So far you have not gotten this far, and so you have a great deal of emphasis put on loving relationships and on communication between male and female energy.

You will find that as you begin to clear your emotional body, you will send out some very strong messages that others will pick up and translate as they see fit. This does not mean that they perceive correctly or that they have an inside track on intuition. It means that they will read you from where they are, and you can only read them from where you are. Once your energy field has cleared, you will be capable of seeing the light and love in "all" on your planet. Nothing will confuse you and polarities will simply move into history.

This is what you are headed into and you are well aware of the darkness you are leaving behind. You are moving in the direction that is most suitable for you, so do not force your direction on the rest of my children. "Each to their own," as you say on earth. Each is allowed his or her own truth and perspective and path to God.

❧

This is how you will see God. You will look upon yourself with wonder and with love. You will look upon yourself with honor and respect. You will look upon yourself with the joy and happiness that comes from knowing that you are the creator. You will find that you do not wish to be less than you are and you will find that you no longer wish to experience limitation. Limitation is good only if you do not wish to be free. Freedom comes from wanting to expand to your fullest capabilities. It is not that you do not wish to expand, it is more that you are stuck and need to let go of some of the weight that you carry in order to move ahead.

You carry so much of what you no longer need that it is suffocating you. It is as though you have come out of your shell, but you still carry your shell for protection. You are no longer in charge when it comes to disposal of your unnecessary garbage. God will lift it from you and you will kick and scream because you will think you are losing, but you are not. You are learning to face you with no pretense and no protection against yourself. You are looking you in the eye without the need to distort what you see. You are beginning the acceptance process.

As you accept all parts of you and as you no longer find need for some parts, they will simply dissolve. They are energy bodies made out of un-dissolved particles of thought and belief placed by judgment. As these parts of you are seen and heard you may decide, once again by thought and belief, to keep them or to discard them. This is the unraveling process, whereby you take off the no longer needed layers and peel you down to a much lighter you. Then, after time when you have realized how much better it is to be without these old patterns and beliefs, you may begin to peel away more of you until you are left stripped of all the garbage you so badly want to hold on to at this time. You are like a child with a security blanket and you are losing it now.

So; when you feel as though you are being taken apart and pulled at and left with no dignity, I want you to remember that you are simply in disguise and the mask is coming off in order to show you who you really are. And who you really are is glorious and wonderful and you have no need to pretense or false dignity. You are so high on the totem pole that it is impossible to get any higher than you. You are also so low that it is impossible to get any lower. You are up, you are down, you are light you are dark, you are love you are fear, you mix it up and call it many other things, but you are the whole show. You play every part and every character and every prop and piece of furniture on stage. You even play the stage and the curtain that falls and the audience and the chairs in the theater... and the theater... and on... and on... and, well, you get the idea.

So now you are focusing on this one you; this one character that you play, and you are clearing this character of your pain and confusion and it is best to take off this costume and remind this character that it is simply a role and do not take it so seriously. It is a game, a part in a big production called "Life on Planet Earth." Soon this production will end and we will go into production on a new program and it will be titled *"Your Life as God."* You will all want a starring role in this new production.

❧❧

*F*or as long as it takes, you will be God. You will know God and you will become the intelligence that is God. You are only sitting in un-intelligence out of choice. You chose ignorance as a method of disguising who you are. Now you are choosing intelligence and knowledge. You are learning that you are not all that you thought and you are learning that you are much more than you ever dreamed. You are highly successful in transmutation and now you have learned that anything that has been transmuted can be changed again and again.

It is not so much that you are learning to start over as it is that you are learning to continue from where you are. It is no longer necessary to die and come back in order to transmute into another form. You may change this form simply by allowing your cells to unload the programming that is breaking them down. Out of this will come life as you have never before experienced it. You have been playing with half a deck and now you are going to begin to play with the full deck. You are going to learn to deal yourself a good hand and you are going to learn to have fun while you are here.

This is how you begin to transcend to a whole new level of life on this planet. You will simply rise to a level of pure pleasure. You will no longer see through your limited vision, so you will have the whole picture which gives you knowledge and awareness, which gives you insight into each situation, which lessens the *need* to judge each situation as a good thing or a bad thing. In wisdom you will find the light and love that you are seeking in order to end conflict. The conflict is in you and the conflict will leave when you no longer find it necessary to disagree with life.

You will find that you will raise you to such a level of complete awareness that you will no longer find it necessary to even argue. Arguing only creates greater conflict and once you begin to see all sides of the situation it will be impossible to argue. It will be as though you are looking at a roadmap that has ten ways or more of getting to your house. Why on earth would you waste your energy arguing over which direction is best when they all reach your destination, which is home?

As you move along your path toward home, you will find that you are unloading and letting go of a great deal of unnecessary programming. This is not the only time you will be asked to let go in order to allow yourself to expand. However, once you get the hang of it, letting go will actually feel good and light and joyful. You will find that many of the situations that you judge as painful and less than wonderful today will actually begin to feel very, very good once you begin to *see* their benefit. This is how you will learn to see the good in all. After a time, each little thing that hurt will turn around and reap a benefit. That job that you lost will become unimportant because the benefits will be a new job you enjoy more. Or maybe the benefit is simply not working and enjoying time in the garden.

It will all make good sense at some point and you will think, "Thank God for not listening when I asked to keep this. It was not as good for me as I thought." You will come to a place where gratitude will flood in and take the place of loss and it will feel so very good. When you get where you're going, you will see why everything happened as it did and you will know how the plan is working and has always been working. You are being led, and pulled, and coerced, and guided, and sometimes you are even being carried out of this mess. Whatever it will take to get you out of your darkness and into your light. You are being moved and shifted and put in place. You are kicking and crying and very upset at God for not making your life better. Here is the good news. God is making your life better and what you are feeling is the cleanup process. You will be shiny bright and ready to rise up right on schedule.

You are the promise and the future and the glory. You are "hope and heaven" all in one. You will become a bright light with thousands and thousands of lives in a single beam. You are everything that is and you are opening yourself up to allow you to be who and what you really are. You are not alone and you never have been. You are being watched and gently led into your own self. You are entering you. You are becoming part of your own creation with full awareness that you are. You are the king and you are the subject. You are also everything in between.

You are shifting now into a new way of viewing all that is, and this shift will allow you to become the creator of your own destiny. You have always been this creator and now you will unveil you so that you know who you are. You will rise to such a level of splendor that the painful shift into light particles will be but a flicker, a moment of spasm that is briefly remembered as you move into your greatness. This is that moment, that instant of birth. The head comes out and the eyes will open and it will take a moment to adjust. You are so comfortable in the confines of the womb. It feels safe and you do not wish to leave, but leave you must. This is simply the first step toward your life as light.

∿

You are now moving to a pivotal point in your creation. You are moving to a place that is not as you are accustomed to being. You have found that you will be most compatible with those who accept how you are and it is good to be accepted. Acceptance leads to loving essence and you do not feel pushed at to be anything but who and what you are. As you move into the turning point which will allow for acceptance, you will see how you have actually entered a phase of loving your own ability to be you. You will see how you are not only happy to be you, you are no longer afraid to be who you are.

This is grace. This phase of "acceptance of self despite what others may or may not accept," is you stepping forward in grace. You are not only stepping into grace, you will begin to move with grace as you will be moving ahead and not trying to take others with you. You will let go gracefully and you will move ahead gracefully.

This will be accomplished by you taking God by the hand and loving God enough to allow God to lead you home. Grace will allow you to slip into a state of total trust that is free of denial and totally accepting. It is your time to move ahead and your time to be this new you who is seeing, and therefore living, from a whole new perspective.

You are no longer struggling with life; you are now in a state of grace which means simply that you accept life as it comes and you flow with life. You are not here to deny and to struggle. You are here to move gracefully through and to see the whole picture as an experience. It was never meant to be judged. It was only meant to be.

As far as one knows, one does not simply exist to be a human. No one so far has come simply to be human. Most of you came for a purpose and that purpose got lost in the way you reacted to the experience of matter. Most of you came with a direct blueprint for a specific intent. This is the beginning of you being who you are. You came to be a specific piece to the makeup of the whole. You came to be the one who is being put in their right place. This means that you no longer feel the need to be outside of creation. You came to be part of creation and it is okay to partake of this creation.

You are not here to sit and judge how this should

be or how that should be. You are here to be a part of creating and enjoying what you have created. You may accept your creation as beautiful or you may turn it into something else. This is your choice for whatever reasons you wish to use. You will find that the more you enjoy your creation the better you begin to create. As you begin to create with greater and greater intent toward love, your creation becomes greater with love. This is the process of creating and, at this moment, you are creating your own self. You are becoming from what you were. You are changing from the old you into a new loving essence that is love.

You will find that as you create this new you, you may begin to feel a little lost and a little out of step with those you once felt so connected to. This is you moving and changing and growing. Think of yourselves as flowers in a giant flower bed. Some of you are only four inches high and close to the ground. This is beautiful to see and creates a lovely ground cover. Some of you are six inches high and are brightly colored and you are having fun hanging out together and waiting for the promised rain to help you grow even taller.

Then there are those who have reached a good twelve inches all on their own and they are proud of their height and talk together about their great progress. Then we have one or two who have decided to *stretch* as high as possible and they are a good twelve inches above the rest. It is difficult at this height to maintain balance and it is difficult to stand in clusters as the length of the stem makes for waving in the breeze. A good strong wind could move you easily and this is why you do not feel confident and connected to the others.

You are moving into a time of separation and growth. You will find that it is no longer necessary to huddle in groups. You are becoming different pieces of a giant puzzle and as you begin to reshape you to become the piece that you are, you will no longer feel the need to be the same shape and size that the other pieces may be. Each piece is different and each piece has its purpose. You all have a purpose or you would not be here. Ground cover for a flower bed is just as beautiful as the tallest flower in the garden. And all the flowers in between actually assist the tallest flowers so when the wind is strongest they have a shorter flower to lean on. Creation is perfect and creation is balanced. You all have your part to play and it is okay to enjoy your own way of doing your part.

Do not be so afraid of displeasing others, for others will only tell you what they want or need for the part that they play. You are you and you know who you are and how you got here. The more you lean on you and use your own guidance the more you will know who you really are.

❧

So far it is good to know how you live for yourself and not for others. You are doing what you want and learning to be more you. You are learning that it is most enjoyable to be the one who is flowing and unconcerned with outcomes. It is good to know how you find joy in lack of resistance. This is peace and calm, no resisting, no conflict, no big trauma.

You will find that once you learn to handle a life of low excitement with little fission and resistance, you will be very happy to experience joy in great quantities. Joy will come in simple pleasures and simple techniques. You will not need so much zing to get you excited about life. You will find that your zing will begin to calm, and your need for shooting chemicals through your body to excite your body will greatly discharge itself. You will become an observer with no great need to participate in exciting games. This will be calming and most enjoyable. Yes, it is thrilling to win and accomplish, but it is also good to keep your energy at a level you can handle.

You can handle love if you do not push it to become something else. Love is what you are and essence is not what you are. You are the creator and you do not have partial authority over creation. It is all yours and you have the ability to make it what you wish. In turning everything into excitement, you shoot your energy out and you push you into situations you would normally not push you into. You are getting the zing which feels good to you because you are programmed to love and accept and honor fear. Fear puts out the rush of hormones to protect you from danger. When you "rush" from excitement, you literally "rush" around inside of you and break down more and more resistance to adrenaline pumping through you. Then you must constantly find a new high or a new project to get excited over.

You are simply stimulating and re-stimulating your body, as though you were plugging you into a light socket in order to watch the sparks fly as you short-circuit or overload. This is stimulation. There are many ways to stimulate the senses and basically what you are doing is moving your energy so that you can "feel." You are numb to feeling as you are numb to who you are. You will find that as you begin to wake up to who you are you will require less and less stimulation to feel alive. You will feel that you are quite content to watch the others discover how to feel by jumping out of planes, or whatever they choose for excitement.

Know that when your body comes into balance, you will need less and less stimulation, as you will be constantly alive with your own life force. You will be constantly moving and tuning in to other bodies and exchanging messages telepathically. If you are at this level now you may not require greater circuitry input and this may make you feel very boring. You are not boring, you simply "feel." Feeling is like a charge, and the more "aware" you are of feeling, the greater activity that goes on within you. This may be stimulation enough and you may wish to walk through life softly in order to keep life flowing through you at a steady pace.

You see, life does flow through you and life does move through all of creation and back to the creator. You have a great deal to learn about life and how you *use* it to be creator. You will find that you not only live, you die and live through it. You flow through life and life flows through you and you are life and life is you. You are coming to a point in your evolution that will teach you to focus on this flow. In other words, you will get down to business. Instead of sending your energy out and about to create excitement, you will begin to follow your energy through its path within you. You will become "in touch" with who you are and the energy that is you.

You are in your infancy stage now so, of course, you are flinging yourself all over and trying to discover how far you can fling yourself. Now is the time for coming back into you. You will find that, as you return, you build reserves of energy to be used in the birthing process. God is being born in matter and this energy will not be excitement. This energy will be wonder!

☙❧

For the first time I will tell you about God. God is not a man. God is not a spirit. God is all things and yet nothing. God begins and ends with each of you and yet God is so much more. God is life force, God is breath, and God is love, God is air, God is earth, God is all that is and all that is not. You are God and your neighbor is God. Your house is God and your car is God. You are God and the minister in your church is God. The gang member is God and the congressman is God. It is all God. Nothing is or ever will be outside of God. All information is God and all innocence is God. All trivia is God and all power is God. From the smallest to the largest, from the tallest to the shortest, from the brightest to the darkest, it is all God. There is nothing that is not God so nothing exists outside of God.

God is not human and God is not spirit in that God cannot be bound to or limited by definition. God is pure in that God possesses only the pure. The pure is clean and open. It is God who is clean and open. It is God who is no longer accepted and it is God who is being denied. You are clean and open and pure the moment you accept that you are. You are pure the moment you realize that you are. It is as though your story is being written as you go, and you have not yet written the part that tells how you discover your true identity as pure love and you live happily ever after.

You will find that as you begin to discover more and more of who you are, you will be more and more of who you are. You *act* as you are told you are. If you are told repeatedly that you are stupid, you will begin to act like you are stupid. If you are told repeatedly that you are beautiful, you will begin to believe you are and you will begin to act like you are. If you are told often enough that you are the love and the light and the God that you are, you may just begin to believe that you are. Repetition is a very good teaching tool so I will continue to repeat myself over and over again until you get me; until you become God in all his glory and wisdom and light. It will not be long now. You are coming very close to knowing and after knowing comes accepting and after accepting comes merging into you; becoming you; becoming all that you know you are and doing it from a conscious state.

You have worked in the dark for too long and now it is time to turn on the lights and know what you have been doing. You are learning to transform matter into light. You are transforming into light. You, God, are creating you as you go. You, God, are making you up as you go and you are also being made up as you think the thoughts that create the creation. The creation is flowing backwards into the creator and the creator is moving into the creation. One and the same. God is you, you are God. God and his creation are one. No one is outside and no one is inside. It is in the making. God is coming in as he thinks his way in.

Thought flows and projects as it goes and thought is all that you are. Thought came from God and God is all that you are. The thought that is, is rolling and spinning a web. It is in creator and in creation. It is one and the same. No one went anywhere. The thought did not leave in order to become whole. The thought simply is and movement simply is. It is still in place and still waiting to become.

Thought moves within the creator and thought is creation. In this way thought and creator are one and the same. The thought is moving in and of itself and this is creation in and of itself. Creator moves thought but thought has its own movement. Thought does not require creator to move in order for thought to move. Thought moves on its own and tells creator what it is doing. Creator then knows what creation, or thought, is about. This causes creator to believe that thought is separate; however, thought is not separate. As a matter of fact, thought is right inside creator were all begins.

You are creator and you are creation. Your thought is that of creation and creator at the same moment. When creator begins to realize that thought is in him, he will know that all movement is his movement. He will know that he moves in and out of his own self in order to achieve motion and movement which is time. There is no time, but creation believes that time is necessary in order to perceive itself. As you begin to learn how you are doing all of this, you will decide to stop pretending that there is anything at all outside of you.

꧁꧂

*F*or the very first time you are beginning to become what you have always been. You are coming into your own and you are coming into you. You are being stretched to hold more of you. You are your own light and you are being put in you. You are being injected with God as you would be injected with a drug. You are coming alive with light and you will know more than you have in eons. You will be so open to new thought and new information that you will become new thought and information.

You are the intelligence of the universe and you are becoming all that you are. Think of this vast memory bank that carries all information of all creation. It is you. You are the memory and the insight to recall memory. You are the information and the intelligence to create from the information. You are all that is and you are still becoming all that is. You are superficial and you are very deep. You are also all layers in between. You are the beginning and the end and the entire circle that does not end. Everything that is or can be is you.

You will find that you are very, very big and yet very, very small. You are so insignificant as to be a speck that may not even show up from certain perspectives and yet you take up all time and space. How can you be all of these? You are super intelligence without boundaries. You may go on and on or you may withdraw into you. You may continue to push outward and expand or you may push inward and expand in that direction. Absolutely everything is possible and everything is part of you. You are only becoming aware of what already is and what has always been. You are not here to be dumb unless you wish to be. You are not here to be smart unless you wish to be. You are here to live only if you wish to live. You are here to die only if you wish to die.

You are everything and anything that you wish to be. You may expand and grow or you may wither in place. Every part must be played out, so you get to volunteer for whatever part you wish to play. You may even change roles in the middle of the play or you may play out the same role over and over again. It is for you, so do it your way. Life is yours, so do what you want with your life and do not do what you do not wish to do. It is just that simple. If you don't like going in one direction then turn and go in another. It is your choice and, as Liane has told her friends,

"It all leads to God because there is no place else to go."

So; if you choose to go to God, you win, and if you do not choose to go to God, you win. You cannot lose because you cannot 'not' go to God, because you are it already. This is the biggest game of tag that you will ever play and you are hiding and seeking your own self. You have always played both roles and now you are simply becoming "aware" of the fact that it is all you. You are one!

⁂

You are not going to like being God. You will find it too liberal and to nonrestrictive. You will be "free" to be and do as you choose and you will no longer be limited to rules. This frightens you. To be free is so new to you that you are not sure you want the responsibility of your freedom. If you are free and make all of your own choices, you cannot blame another for your pain or any other emotional tragedy. You are God and you choose to create in such a manner as to create pain or not create pain.

You may see all situations as joyful or you may see them as painful. It is up to you and it always has been; only now you are *aware* of your creations and how you have chosen to evolve. So, let's let go of blame and begin to accept responsibility for our own messes. Just say to yourself, "Yes, this is a big one, I wonder what I am going to learn from it," and go on your merry way. Do not try to pin the blame on the one who is cooperating in your plan to teach you how to see life differently. If you did not need the lesson, why do you think you would create it? Do you create just to entertain, or punish, or perhaps to show you how you do not use your powers as well as you could? Do you learn by not experiencing through the emotional body or do you seem to learn a lot by emotional evolution?

So; do you think maybe you are in such a rush to get to where you wish to be that you push yourself by setting up lessons to teach you to let go of this or that, to allow you to see how good it is to be less matter; or do you think you make you out to be some sort of dunce who never gets it right, just to evolve into your anger so you might discharge anger enough to free you in that area? Or maybe you are just unlucky and so you create situations that are unlucky, like being on a bridge when an earthquake shakes it down into a river of frozen water. Does this type of creation mean you are unlucky or could there be meaning for it? Could it be that you were showing others how it is okay to die, or could it be that you simply decided to get lucky and go to the light through death?

Choices are wide and varied and there are millions and millions of reasons for them. As a matter of fact, there are so many reasons for choices made that you could never retrace far enough back to unravel all the reasons that were decided upon, from lifetime to lifetime, and from soul incarnation to soul incarnation. So, begin to simply know that you are unraveling you enough to begin creating from consciousness, as well as unconsciousness. You are beginning to know who you are and how you want to be.

You are allowing all of the unwanted programming to fall away and you are emerging into your own self. You are finding that as you emerge you are confronted with new issues that will allow this new you to make conscious choices as to direction and flow of life. These new choices will be guided from light, as light is moving out of you and into you at the same moment.

As you grow and become aware, you begin to pulsate and to be very much in the light. Light is moving in and out of you as well as around you. The more you allow intelligence in, the more you become intelligence. It is almost like becoming a star. You are growing from a tiny speck into a brilliant light body. You will create greater brilliance the greater you become. The more light you are the more light you shed. You become so big and so bright that you are shining outward billions and billions of light-years. You, the tiny spark that is you, can grow to this vastness and greatness. Just by shining your light you grow more and more bright. Just as a life that is going out becomes more and more dim, those who are coming in become more and more bright.

You have a bright future and you have an even brighter present, you just cannot see it. I will teach you to see the brightness in the moment so that you will no longer project into future creations for your gratification. You will begin to see how bright and wonderful today is without a care nor a worry for tomorrow. This is when you begin to shed or give off light. You will like this phase of your preparation for godhood. You will most enjoy sending out and receiving messages of joy and rapture. This will be discussed in our next book titled *God Lives*. For now I bid you all a fond adieu, with all the joy and adoration that you too become totally magnificent in your true identity as God. You are a light of great beauty and love. You hold this entire universe together and you don't even remember that you do.

You will remember, and when you do you will grow with such astonished glee at the simple knowingness that you did it all and then you forgot all.

God's Pen

I first heard the voice of God in 1988. I was sitting in my back yard reading a book when this big booming voice interrupted with, "I am God and I will not come to you by any other name." I felt like the voice was everywhere – inside of me as well as in the sky around me. I was so frightened that I ran in my bedroom to hide.

This was not the first time that I heard voices. I had been communicating with my own spirit guide or soul for about a year. I guess my depth of fear regarding God, and all that he represented to me at the time, was just too much.

I spent two days trying to avoid the voice of God, which was patiently waiting for me to respond. By the second day I was exhausted from lack of sleep and decided to give in and talk with him. This turned out to be the greatest gift and best decision of my life.

The first book, *God Spoke through Me to Tell You to Speak to Him*, shows my evolution from communicating with my soul to communicating with the Big Guy. It took a couple years for me to be comfortable communicating with God. My fear of a punishing God was big! That has most definitely changed and I now think of God as my partner and best friend.

In the beginning the voice of God would wake me in the middle of the night and tell me it was time to write. He said I had promised to do this work (I assumed he was talking about the soul/spirit me). I would drag myself up to a sitting position and watch in amazement as my hand flew across the page, while I tried to keep up by reading what was being written.

It was always so much fun to wake up the next morning and grab my notebook to see what God had written during the night. After some time the voice stopped waking me and I became comfortable picking up my pen and writing for God first thing in the morning. I think in the beginning I had to be awakened while still semi-conscious from sleep so I wouldn't object too much to the information that was being channeled through me.

As I grew less and less afraid (and more trusting) of God, he was able to communicate greater information. Some of the information is quit controversial, but I felt it important to just let it be and not censor it. I present the writings here to you as they were given to me. I have edited a little (mostly the more personal information regarding myself) and I have used a pen name for privacy reasons. I asked God for a good pen name and he guided me to Liane which (I was told) in Hebrew means "God has answered."

At one point I became a little concerned about my sanity in all this, so I went to a hypnotherapist to find out what I was doing. Under hypnosis I saw this incredibly huge beam of light with a voice coming from within it. It was a giant "loving light" and felt so comforting and kind. It felt like that's where I came from. After that I stopped worrying about my sanity. If this is crazy, I think it's a very good kind of crazy to be....

In loving light, Liane

www.ingramcontent.com/pod-product-compliance
Lightning Source LLC
Chambersburg PA
CBHW021053090426

42738CB00006B/321